UNCLE DUNKLE AND DONNIE

Fractured Fables by DAWS BUTLER

Co-written, Edited & Illustrated by Joe Bevilacqua

Uncle Dunkle and Donnie
© 2009 Myrtis & Charles Butler, Joe Bevilacqua. All Rights Reserved.
"Preface" copyright © 2009 by Mark Evanier
"Foreword" copyright © 2009 by Joe Bevilacqua
"Man of Many Talents" copyright © 2008 by The Delaware-Hudson Canvas
Illustrations copyright © 2009 by Joe Bevilacqua
Audio Book copyright © 2009 by Joe Bevilacqua

All illustrations are copyright of their respective owners, and are also reproduced here in the spirit of publicity. Whilst we have made every effort to acknowledge specific credits whenever possible, we apologize for any omissions, and will undertake every effort to make any appropriate changes in future editions of this book if necessary.

No part of this book may be reproduced in any form or by any means, electronic, mechanical, digital, photocopying or recording, except for the inclusion in a review, without permission in writing from the publisher.

Published in the USA by:
BearManor Media
P O Box 71426
Albany, Georgia 31708
www.bearmanormedia.com

ISBN 1-59393-133-9

Printed in the United States of America.

Book design by Darlene Swanson of Van-garde Imagery, Inc.
Cover design, illustration Photoshop work by Lorie B. Kellogg, waterlogg.com

UNCLE DUNKLE AND DONNIE

Fractured Fables by
DAWS BUTLER

Dedicated to Myrtis Butler,
who has treated me like a son.

DAWS BUTLER

September 4, 1980

A word or two about Joe Bevilacqua (Joe Bev).

I have been his mentor during his 'important' growing up years - the last six or so.

He wrote me via HANNA-BARBERA STUDIOS when he was a kid in High School - planning and executing assembly entertainments - special material and performances.

Even then, he had an advanced 'writer's' and 'actor's' sense. He and a buddy came up with parodies on current Television Programs - succinct and with a bite I thought to be beyond their creative years.

He sent me cartoons he had done. Cassettes with his 'characterizations' .. which, at time, left much to be desired - they were like castings with not enough of the 'flash' removed! ... but we worked.

I recognized a rare commodity in Joe - 'Raw Talent.' I find it occasionally but not often - It is a seedling that with the proper nurturing can only grow.

I sent Joe monologues, dialogues, parodies - the fruit of my work-shop curriculum. He would study them and send back - on cassettes - his interpretations .. which were above average -- instead of the obvious, run-of-the-mill interpretations I sometimes experienced in my work-shop -- Joe's showed insight and sophisticated evaluation.

In our 'over-the-miles' relationship, I could literally feel Joe's growth. He didn't stand still - he rested on no laurels. I was miserly with my compliments. When he got one, he knew it was deserved - he was made to appreciate and work for a compliment.

This sounds like a PR release! It's just that for the past seven years I have conducted a work-shop for mostly professional actors and writers - who needed polish - considered Joe to be a potential 'professional.'

I had to scrape off some of the 'flash.'

In College he has worked in production, stage-craft - straight and character acting - and expressed the desire to 'know it all.' And to participate where he was needed - sometimes in several categories.

His shaping and shading of words - his attention to the orchestration of whatever piece he is performing has come to an enrichment of viable, believable expression.

I think Joe is good. Now he needs work and experience - a chance to show the fruits of his study.

He has energy and sensitivity and drive - and he is aware of the 'word' and its power.

What more can I say? I wouldn't bet him to Place or Show - but to Win.

Sincerely,

Daws Butler

PREFACE

by Mark Evanier, Writer-Historian

I used to stare at his mouth. I'm sorry but I did.

I grew up on the voice of Daws Butler, hearing him in Warner Brothers cartoons, Jay Ward cartoons, Hanna-Barbera cartoons, Stan Freberg records . . . all my favorite things. So when I got to know him and he'd talk to me, I couldn't believe it. That voice was coming out of that mouth . . . the mouth of a human being. One of the humanest of all beings I have ever met, for that matter. He was a lovely man . . . adored by all, respected by all. And a superb teacher.

Put it this way: Daws was as fine a teacher as he was an actor . . . and you all know what a fine actor he was. Those who got to study with him (like Joe Bevilacqua) were privileged . . . and talented, coming and going.

Students were talented when they went in. Daws wouldn't take just anybody. He had to see some potential in you. Today, there are voice coaches who'll accept and encourage any student who can pay . . . and they charge 10-20 times what Daws did.

Students were more talented when they went out. It wasn't just the lessons. It was being around Daws.

His very presence in the room made you feel more creative and commanded that you rise somewhat closer to his level. You could never be as good as him – that was a "given" – but you could earn the right to share a microphone for a little while.

The Uncle Dunkle scripts in this book show what he expected of his pupils. They are not mindless exposition, easily read by anyone who can master the basic vowel sounds. They're full of personality, expression, attitude and color. They demand performers who know where the jokes are and they aren't just in the words. They're in the characters . . .not so much what they say as how they say it. To do justice to these skits requires not just reading but acting. Good acting.

Fortunately, like I said, Joe Bev got to study with the master . . . to join that long parade of folks who came out more talented than when they went in. Joe learned from the very best and you can hear him putting all that to work in his performances, especially when he assumes Daws's old, difficult task of doing both parts in a dialogue, playing Abbott to his own Costello. A lot of performers just don't have the talent or the guts (or both) to pull that off.

Those of us who loved (and still love) Daws are grateful to Joe for all his endeavors that keep the name alive. This fine collection of the works of Butler and Bevilacqua is yet another in a long list.

UNCLE DUNKLE AND DONNIE

Foreword by Joe Bevilacqua

The first time I participated in a Daws Butler acting workshop, I was a gawky 17-year-old with braces. It was the summer of 1976 and it was my first trip to Southern California. Daws's workshop came about at a time when the great voice actor, who had created so many memorable characters with Stan Freberg, Tex Avery, Bill Hanna and Joe Barbera, Jay Ward and Bob Clampett (to name a few), was rarely working. Out of a combination of frustration, boredom and the desire to pass on what he knew, Daws set up a long table in his Beverly Hills home studio/garage and invited young would-be actors to come over and read scripts he had written.

I ended up part of this lucky group because I had written a letter to Daws the year before which eventually led to Daws listening to a cassette of voices and story ad-libs I performed called "Willoughby and the Professor" and dubbing himself my personal mentor.

Here I was sitting at the table next to the man who had pretty much created the personalities of Yogi Bear, Huckleberry Hound, Mr. Jinx, Dixie, Quick-Draw McGraw, Baba Looey, Snagglepuss, Super Snooper, Blabbermouse, Augie Doggie, Wally Gator, Lippy the Lion, Elroy Jetson, Peter Potamus, Cap'n Crunch, and dozens more.

At Daws's invitation, my mom, sister and I flew to Beverly Hills, California, from New Jersey. They sat off to the side and watched as I tried to keep up with the others in the group, many of whom, including Corey Burton, Earl Kress, Billy Simpson, Tony Pope and Pat Parris, had already worked as professional voice actors. We read a few dramatic scripts Daws had written - subtle quiet dialogs about interpersonal relationships, not cartoony at all. Some of these scripts can be found in the book Scenes for Actors and Voices, which I edited with Ben Ohmart, published by BearManor Media (www.bearmanormedia.com).

Then, Daws pulled out a script he had just written called "Punky Possum's Mud Bath." It featured kindly old Uncle Dunkle telling a story to his nephew, Donnie. We followed that with a reading of "Sticky Wicket," another Uncle Dunkle story. I read several parts in them and was pretty awful, but the scripts themselves were beautifully written and I became fond of the characters immediately.

In some ways reminiscent of Jay Ward's "Fractured Fairy Tales" and "Aesop and Sons" cartoons in which Daws had acted in as part of the *Rocky and Bullwinkle* TV show, Uncle Dunkle and Donnie is uniquely Daws Butler. In fact, Daws had begun developing the characters and premises years before the Ward cartoons of the late 1950s and early '60s. In 1947, Daws wrote and voiced a children's record for Disney, featuring "Bongo the Bear" and "Little Hiawatha," narrated by Jack Benny's announcer Don Wilson. "Little Hiawatha" was based on a 1937 Disney *Silly Symphony* and "Bongo the Bear" was released theatrically in 1947 as part of Disney's *Fun and Fancy Free*, along with "Mickey and the Beanstalk," in neither of which Daws's voice appears. More records featuring Daws's version of classic stories followed, including "Chirpy the Cricket" and "Happy the Grasshopper."

Throughout the late 1940s and early 1950s, Daws also wrote and voiced a number of children's records which were original in character and plot, featuring some of the characters that would later populate the world of Uncle Dunkle, such as Sleepy Ole Mr. Toad, Peppy Possum (later called Punky Possum) and Teddy Turtle (who grew up to become Theodore Turtle). To give the most complete picture of the character's origins, these prototype stories are included in this book, alongside the official Dunkle stories, with the generic narrator of the originals replaced by Dunkle himself. They are "The Flying Turtle" and "Peppy Possum."

As an interesting side note: the premise behind "The Flying Turtle" and "Theodore the Turtle" call to mind another 1960s TV cartoon, "Tutor Turtle" with which Daws was not involved. It is unknown who came up with the idea of a dissatisfied turtle magically transformed by a reptile wizard, but Daws put out a record of "The Flying Turtle" in the early 1950s.

Between 1976 and 1988, Daws wrote hundreds of scripts for his acting workshop. Many of these featured Uncle Dunkle and Donnie. During that time, we both tried to sell them as an animated cartoon series. Joe Barbera liked them and shopped them to the networks, without success. Jay Ward tried unsuccessfully as well. The days of charming animal stories had long passed. Most rejection comments centered on the clever, sophisticated language and how children would not understand some of the words. Daws's reply was simple. "They'll learn the words," just like every child who'd ever watched a Warner Brothers, Hanna-Barbera or Jay Ward cartoon, in the 1930s through the early 1960s, before Saturday morning TV became a babysitter and long before 24-hour cable channels.

After Daws had a stroke that left him struggling with written language for a time, I wrote a series of Dunkle tales, under Daws's editorial guidance, in short-story format. In 1986, a collection of these stories won a New Jersey state children's literature award. The short stories, with titles such as "Terrance Tiger and the Thunderstorm," "The Enchanted Train," "The Security Guard Mouse," and "The Worm, the Chicken and the Weasel," are not included in this collection. However, a number of Dunkle scripts I wrote are in this volume, including "Bigelow Bee and the Honey Factory," "Dunkle's Old Jalopy," "Helpful the Dwarf," "Rapunzel and the Bandit," "Sherlock Snail Finds a Home."

Daws edited these and we used them in his workshop, during one of which I had the pleasure once of hearing Daws as Donnie and Penny Singleton (Blondie, Jane Jetson) as Aunt Rapunzel reading my script, "Bigelow Bee and the Honey Factory." I performed Bigelow Bee. Unfortunately, no recording of this exists.

The Uncle Dunkle stories in this book fall into five categories (with some overlap): talking animal fables, dreams, enchanted objects, deconstructed fairy tales and history, and nonsense. Many of these stories involve a child figure learning individuality and self-worth.

You will note that Daws wrote two versions of "Little Red Riding Who?" – one with Uncle Dunkle and the other with Aunt Rapunzel telling the story. Both are included in this volume.

In illustrating this book, I tried to emulate a vintage classic Hanna-Barbera style. Some of these were featured as part of the 2008 ArtsWE exhibit in Ellenville, New York.

A newly-recorded audio book of all the Uncle Dunkle stories in this collection, with me performing all the characters is available at www.bearmanoraudio.com. It also features me performing sound effects, my wife, Lorie Kellogg's eagle calls on "Rapunzel and the Bandit", and my musical score and songs performed by The Paul Salomone Jazz-Trio, Joe Gatto and Julian Baker.

As De Facto keeper of the Daws Butler Archives, I plan on releasing more soon. The man was prolific. He himself recorded a number of "Dunkles" doing all the voices. Daws's son, Chas Butler (as a teen) played drums on Daws's version of "The Magic Drums." There are recordings of Daws and Chas (as a young child) reading "Jack and the Beans Talk," first with Daws playing Dunkle as Yogi Bear and then Mr. Jinx. And another of me performing "Punky Possum's Mud Bath," with June Foray, Corey Burton and Nancy Cartwright during a tribute to Daws at the Glendale Auditorium in Glendale, CA, in 2003. And a lot more treasures! Dunkle stories may even end up animated on your TV, Internet and Ipods screens someday.

You can hear a lot more Daws Butler, Mel Blanc, Paul Frees, June Foray, Walt Disney, Uncle Dunkle and rare cartoon audio, interviews, and music on my radio show, "Cartoon Carnival," which airs seven days a week at 6:00 p.m. (EST), 5:00 p.m. (CTL) 3:00 p.m. (PDT), on the Shokus Radio Network: www.shokusradio.com.

To read further about Daws Butler's amazing life and career, including more about Uncle Dunkle and Donnie, check out the authorized biography, Daws Butler: Characters Actor, which I co-wrote with Ben Ohmart, and Scenes for Actors and Voices, scripts from Daws Butler's workshop, both published by BearManor Media (www.bearmanormedia.com).

Now it is time to enter the fantastic world of talking animals and fractured fables created by Daws Butler. Read them to yourself, read them out loud, read them to your children, follow along with the audio book, play the audio book for your kids as bedtime stories, perform them for and with friends, read them around a table with a group, stage them as children's theater, create your own "Daws Butler Workshop". Spread the joy that is Uncle Dunkle and Donnie!

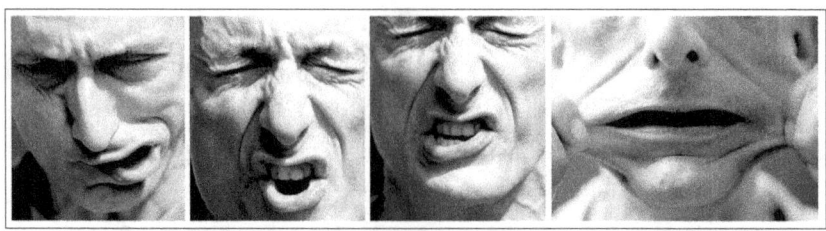

Joe Bevilacqua demonstrates some of the faces he makes when creating his character's voices. Photos by Chris Pike.

JOE BEVILACQUA: A MAN OF MANY TALENTS

By Sharlene Hartman

Joe Bevilacqua is one of those enviable people in the arts, who always seem to be actively using their talent. If he's not currently cast in a project, he'll produce a project of his own. His talents run the gamut from drawing detailed cartoons since the age of five, developing and performing voices for cartoon characters and producing 100s of programs for National Public Radio (NPR). He is an award-winning writer, broadcaster, documentarian, and aside from about a dozen more accomplishments he understands quantum physics. And, no matter what project he is involved in, he is quick to state that "Lorie Kellogg, my wife, who came into my life 12 years ago, is the other half of my creative work." In fact, for four years they did a program on XM Satellite Radio called *The Comedy-O-Rama Hour*, which Joe co-wrote, produced, directed, and performed 80-90% of the voices.

"Joe Bev's" been at it since he was three years old, when he started performing for his family; making up characters and mimicking what he saw on TV. At six his family moved from Newark, New Jersey, to a house in the suburbs that had a large attic that wasn't being used. By the time he was 12, Joe had moved upstairs and created his own "fake apartment." He furnished it with any and all furniture that would fit into the room, including a couch and a desk ... and he would go downstairs just to bring his meals up to the attic. "I disassociated myself from my family because they were always arguing, there was always conflict." He also felt he didn't measure up to his father's definition of "a man." It was another time and Joe said, "I was just a little different; I didn't want to play sports, I didn't care about cars ... I was an artsy-fartsy guy."

So Joe found sanctuary in an attic and turned it into his own fantasy world, "where I would draw cartoons, make up funny voices and perform for friends." He even ended up forcing his friends to perform, "if you played with Joe Bev you had to be inventive...we put on shows." And he still has some of those shows recorded on tape.

After seeing a Warner Brothers' cartoon, where Elmer Fudd was a scientist planning to experiment on Bugs Bunny, he decided to make up his own cartoon characters; "a professor with a dumb assistant," thus creating Willoughby and the Professor, characters he still does on the radio today. He made up the voices and created a story, "ad-libbing my way though...nothing was written down." His father gave him a tape recorder with a microphone that had an on/off switch. If he needed time to think, he'd just pause the recording until he could come up with the next line. He ended up recording a number of 30-minute shows, "the length of a one-act play, which is what Radio Theatre does best." He had never heard Radio Theatre, so he thought he was actually "inventing it," sound effects and all.

Having a private "studio," to develop ideas in, paid off big time in high school. His first mentor, Gordon Inverno, of Thomas Aquinas

High School, saw that Joe had talent as an actor, cartoonist, writer and director...and he let Joe "do all kinds of things," including a five-minute weekly satirical news program on the school public address system. Suddenly the girls liked him and "the sports guys didn't think I was so bad ... everything that happens to you in life makes you who you are, so I have no regrets."

At 16, he wrote a letter to Daws Butler, the voice of Yogi Bear and Elroy Jetson among others; both were Hanna-Barbera cartoons (now owned by Warner Brothers), which were Joe's favorite. He told Mr. Butler that he wanted to be a voice actor. Daws tried to discourage Joe with a letter telling him how hard it was. Joe wrote back saying, "I know it's hard but I've been doing this my whole life, this is what I'm going to do." Daws wrote back saying, "You're the first kid that wrote back ... you bounce back well. OK, let's see what you've got."

Joe sent Daws four half-hour Willoughby and the Professor stories. Then Daws sent him back a 30-minute cassette, just talking to Joe and giving him a variety of voices to practice. Daws taught him the "details of elocution, speech and projection" and so much more. For many summers, Joe, his mother and sister traveled to Beverly Hills, to spend time with Daws and his family. He attended Daws' workshops, and later edited a book Daws wrote on his voice methods. Joe became Daws' apprentice, as well as "like a fifth son." His mentor emphasized the importance of voice actors using their whole body as an instrument, "it frees you up." A person's posture and freedom of gesture all help to "develop ways of coloring the sentences. Daws called it 'orchestrating a script, like a conductor orchestrates music.'"

Joe has always enjoyed teaching and mentoring people. He's been a Broadcasting Professor at Marist College, taught Speech at SUNY Ulster, English as a Second Language at his alma mater Kean University, English and Creative Writing at Rutgers University, and he's always worked privately with people wanting his coaching expertise in voice-work and acting. In fact, he has clients that he coaches over the phone.

The principles that Joe learned in Daws' workshops are what Joe passes on to his students today. In order to accommodate more students, Joe has started having weekly workshops. The people that attend range from beginners to accomplished professionals. "A professional in the class usually raises the level for everyone, everybody learns from everybody." Private coaching is good for fine tuning, "you can chisel away, focus on a particular problem you are trying to improve. But a group session accelerates learning, because you are developing better listening skills which helps you to learn faster ... and everyone is sharing ideas."

Not only aspiring thespians and voice actors can benefit from Joe Bev's workshops. It's an excellent way to improve communication skills, overcome shyness, and help with presentation skills ..."it's all the same tools." Joe says "anybody that's ever worked with me goes away totally energized, doing things that they couldn't imagine they were capable of. We go through enunciation, articulation, and cold-reading techniques. You'll just communicate better. After the first session people go away with more confidence. They did something they thought they couldn't do. We sit around the table with scripts; there is no ego involved and no judgment. It's all supportive. When people keep coming back, it becomes like a club; a safe place to try things, learn, experiment and have fun; and doing it using a method that was developed by a guy who did the happiest, most joyful cartoons that have ever been made."

Find more Joe Bev info at: http://www.joebev.com, http://www.dawsbutler.com, http://www.comedyorama.com

Reprinted from the September 2008 issue of the Delaware-Hudson CANVAS. See the printed article with photos here: http://www.joebev.com/joebev-press/CANVAS-ARTICLE-Joe-Sept08-MED.jpg

CONTENTS

Preface v

Uncle Dunkle and Donnie. vii

Joe Bevilacqua: A Man of Many Talents xii

"A Little Bird Told Me" 1

"Alexander Remembers" 10

"Because Aunt Rapunzel Was There" 14

"Bigelow Bee and the Honey Factory" 20

"Britty the Starfish" 36

"Donnie and the Piggy Bank" 42

"Dunkle's Old Jalopy"...............47

"Helpful the Dwarf".................59

"Humpty-Dumpty's Friend"...........67

"Jack and the Beans Talk"..........75

"Johnny the Giraffe"................80

"Little Red Riding Who?"...........85

"Little Red Riding Who?"...........91

"Malcolm the Old Tire".............98

"Murray the Magpie"...............106

"Penny and Guinnie"...............113

"Peppy Possum"....................120

"Perky the Pig"...................125

"Pete the Pelican"................131

"Punky Possum's Mud Bath".........136

"Rapunzel and the Bandit".........143

"Reddy Robin and the Owl".........152

"Sherlock Snail Finds a Home".....158

"Sticky Wicket"...................163

"The Big Wind"....................169

"The Cherry Tree Caper". 174

"The Enchanted Tape Recorder" 179

"The Flying Turtle" 191

"The Green Cow" 197

"The Lonesome Umbrella" 202

"The Magic Drums" 210

"The Talking Violin" 218

"The Tardy Wedding Guest" 227

"Theodore the Turtle" 232

"Uncle Dunkle and Donnie and Wootsy" 238

"Uncle Dunkle Reveals All" 246

"A LITTLE BIRD TOLD ME"

DUNKLE: Donnie?

DONNIE: Uh-huh?

DUNKLE: When somebody asks you where you got some important piece of information, have you ever said: 'A little bird told me?'

DONNIE: Why would I say that?

DUNKLE: I just wondered. See, sometimes people say that when they don't want to divulge where that important piece of information came from.

DONNIE: Divulge?

DUNKLE: Um.

DONNIE: What does 'divulge' mean?

DUNKLE: It means 'tell.'

DONNIE: Then why didn't you say 'tell?'

DUNKLE: It means the same thing as divulge.

DONNIE: Yeah, but I know what 'tell' means - but I don't know what divulge means.

DUNKLE: You know _now_.

DONNIE: Huh?

DUNKLE: (LAFF) I gotcha!!

DONNIE: Guess you did! That's a pretty sneaky way of teachin' me a new word!

DUNKLE: It's a thing Uncle Dunkle's do - you gotta watch out for us.

DONNIE: You mean, there's more than one Uncle Dunkle?

DUNKLE: There must be! I couldn't stand the responsibility of being the _only_ one!

DONNIE: (CHUCKLE) You're doin' all right so far. (CHANGE) What were you talkin' about before - about a bird?

DUNKLE: I was saying that when a person says 'a little bird told me' ... it's because they don't want to divulge where the information actually came from.

DONNIE: They're tellin' a fib, right?

DUNKLE: Sort of.

DONNIE: They are.

DUNKLE: They are, sort of. I'm really getting more involved in this than I meant to be. What I wanna tell you about is not what a little bird told me, but what I told a little bird.

DONNIE: Was it a fib?

DUNKLE: No . . . it was a sparrow.

DONNIE: (CHUCKLE)

DUNKLE: . . . and this sparrow did a very noble thing - performed a valuable service. He did it for a friend of mine - this man who retired from his job. He'd worked hard all his life and now he figgered he'd earned the right to take it easy. His name was Herman Haha.

DONNIE: That's a funny name.

DUNKLE: Yeah, sort of. We were talkin' one day, Herman Haha and me, and Herman said:

HERMAN: D'Artanyan, I am sore perplexed. I never had a hobby. I just worked. I never learned to play golf . . . or tennis . . . or chess . . . or even tiddlywinks. I did read the rules on tiddlywinks, but I never got around to actually playing it.

DUNKLE: You missed out on a lot of fun. I was a west-coast contender.

HERMAN: Well, now I'm older and retired and I've grown quite plump.

DUNKLE: Fat.

HERMAN: I said 'plump.'

DUNKLE: Well, plump means fat.

HERMAN: Yes, but it doesn't sound as fat as 'fat.' Well, being quite plump, my doctor doesn't want me to involve myself in any activity which is too strenuous, so I have decided to become a bird-watcher! Even though I am near-sighted.

DUNKLE: Well, Donnie - once Herman Haha made up his mind to do something, nothing could change him. I tried to talk him out of the bird-watching idea . . . but not because of his eyes.

DONNIE: Why?

DUNKLE: Bad timing. See, winter was coming on - and all the birds had flown south for the warm weather . . . all the birds, that is, but the sparrow.

DONNIE: Your friend?

DUNKLE: More of an acquaintance, actually . . . see, the sparrow sticks out the winter with the rest of us . . . so, knowing that my friend, Herman . . .

DONNIE: Haha.

DUNKLE: Huh?

DONNIE: Haha.

DUNKLE: What's so funny?

DONNIE: I was just rememberin' Herman's last name . . . Haha.

DUNKLE: It wasn't any laughing matter . . . Herman Haha expecting to go out bird-watching . . . when there wouldn't be any birds.

DONNIE: Except sparrows.

DUNKLE: So what I did, I called on this sparrow acquaintance of mine . . . name of Billingsly. He was way up on top of an elm tree in his nest and couldn't hear me yelling at him, so what I did, I had your Aunt Rapunzel shinny up the tree and tap him on the head . . .

DONNIE: Aw, she did not!

DUNKLE: That's right, she didn't! Of course, she didn't! (BEAT) She tapped him on the <u>shoulder</u> - mighta hurt his little old head!

DONNIE: (QUIETLY) She did not.

DUNKLE: She told him I wanted to ask him something and he flew down to the ground.

DONNIE: How'd Aunt Rapunzel get down to the ground?

DUNKLE: She didn't. She's still up in the tree.

DONNIE: She is not.

DUNKLE: Then I don't know where she is.

DONNIE: She's out in the kitchen . . . right now . . . making mustard fudge.

DUNKLE: She never tells me <u>anything</u>. (UP) Anyway, I told Billingsly I wanted to ask a favor of him . . . I explained about how Herman Haha was gonna do some bird-watching, but there weren't gonna be any pretty or interesting birds around and Billingsly said:

BILLINGSLY: You sure know how to hurt a guy!

DUNKLE: ...but he understood what I meant... and would have accepted my apology if I'd made one... and said he'd help if he could. I said: 'Billingsly; my wife, Rapunzel, has made up dozens of bird costumes that you can put on to fool Herman Haha into thinking he's seeing a whole bunch of different birds!

BILLINGSLY: I don't wish to appear crass - but what's in it for me?

DUNKLE: A cookie fragment.

BILLINGSLY: Now you're talkin'! I don't come cheap, y'know.

DUNKLE: You don't come what?

BILLINGSLY: Cheap! Cheap!

DUNKLE: I'll say one thing, you have a way with chirps. (LAFF) Well, Donnie — Aunt Rapunzel made a little valise for Billingsly's costumes... and Billingsly learned how to imitate the various bird-calls... and I coached Herman Haha on bird-watching techniques. (CHANGE - UP) O.K. Herman, let's see if you got everything! You got the hiking boots - the drab clothes - binoculars - a reference book of the various birds you'll be seeing... and a notebook, to keep track of all the birds you see.

HERMAN: That seems to cover everything.

DUNKLE: Except the salt.

HERMAN: Salt?

DUNKLE: Yeah, salt - to put on a bird's tail if you wanna study him up close.

HERMAN: But what if I can't get up close?

DUNKLE: Then you carry this hard-boiled egg - so the salt won't go to waste.

HERMAN: ...and I'll need a camera - so I can ask the birdie to watch the birdie! (CHUCKLES)

DUNKLE: So Herman was all set... and he started out on his first expedition... Billingsly, the sparrow, flew on ahead of him and changed into all of his various costumes - he had to work fast because Herman was a big man and took long strides. Before long, poor Billingsly was exhausted. He climbed out of the robin costume he'd been wearing... and tried to catch his breath.

BILLINGSLY: (PANTS)

HERMAN: (UP) Why, that's just an old sparrow - I won't even write down that I saw him... he's not important!

DUNKLE: ... and Herman walked on through the forest, leaving poor little Billingsly behind. As he went deeper and deeper into the forest, he became hopelessly lost.

HERMAN: (FRIGHTENED) I'm as lost as a bagel in a Chinese restaurant!

DUNKLE: But there was no one to laugh at his joke - and there was no laugh-track... and night was coming on! Billingsly had been following him silently, rather annoyed at the snide way Herman had referred to his ordinariness - but as he got closer to Herman and saw the worried look on his face, he drew the words 'follow me' on a piece of bark...

and holding it in his beak, he flew down so that Herman could see it.

DONNIE: ...and did Herman see it?

DUNKLE: He did... and he said:

HERMAN: Hmm, here's a little sparrow with a sign, which offers me the option of following him. Lead on, little sparrow!... and I wish to apologize for the unkind remark I made about you a while back .. of all the beautiful birds I saw today, you're the only one who helped me. I'm putting your name on the top of my bird-list. I'll just jot that down:
 'Sparrow - description - ugly, but well-meaning'... that should do it.

BILLINGSLY: ...and I was out people-watching today – and you're the only people I saw... so I will put you down on my list... I'll just say... 'One man – description... fat.'

HERMAN: Plump.

BILLINGSLY: Fat.

HERMAN: You think I'm fat?

BILLINGSLY: You *are* fat.

HERMAN: ...and you're ugly.

BILLINGSLY: ...and you're still lost! I'll see you around!

HERMAN: Wait! Wait! Actually, you're beautiful... and you're right. I *am* fat!

DUNKLE: ...so Billingsly lead Herman Haha out of the forest - and

Herman invited his newfound sparrow friend to dinner - and gave him bird-seed Stroganoff... and you know what Billingsly brought for dessert?

DONNIE: Sure. The cookie fragment.

DUNKLE: The cookie fragment!

DUNKLE & DONNIE: (CHUCKLE)

"ALEXANDER REMEMBERS"

DUNKLE: Say, Donnie - do you remember what I told you yesterday?

DONNIE: Let's see - uh - Oh, yeah . . . um . . . you told me to remember that today, you were gonna ask me if I remembered what you told me, yesterday!!

DUNKLE: Very good! Funnily enough, I had a good reason for askin' you to remember that I was gonna ask ya if you remembered what I told ya yesterday!

DONNIE: Uh, Uncle Dunkle - I'm gettin' kinda mixed up. What was the good reason?

DUNKLE: The subject of today's story (LAFF) - it's about forgettin'.

DONNIE: . . . but I remembered!

DUNKLE:	Sure, you did - but Alexander didn't! Y'see, Alexander was a little elephant - well, that is, as little as an elephant can be! (LAFF) Even when they're babies . . . uh.. they're not very little! Now, there's a thing that people say about elephants - that they never forget. Well, that's the strange thing about Alexander, Donnie - he always forgot everything his mother told him!
MAMA:	Alexander! How much is two and two?
ALEX:	I forget.
MAMA:	Forget what?
ALEX:	. . . Uh . . . whatever it was you asked me.
MAMA:	Once more, Alexander - how much is two and two?
ALEX:	I forget.
MAMA:	The answer is four. Now will you try to remember that?
ALEX:	Remember what?
MAMA:	Alexander, elephants - large and small - are supposed to remember things. You don't remember anything!!!
ALEX:	'cause I forget!
MAMA:	And what did I say?
ALEX:	About what?
DUNKLE:	Well, this went on every day, Donnie. Poor Alexander's mother didn't know what to do. The other animals of the forest got annoyed with Alexander and his poor memory, too - and they weren't very friendly. In fact, Alexander

	didn't have any friends - so he used to take long, solitary walks every day. But Alexander's mother had faith that someday . . . something or somebody that Alexander cared about, would trigger his memory - and he would live up to the elephant's creed - never forgetting anything! Well, one day, as he was setting out on one of his long, solitary jaunts, his mother cautioned him about something . . .
MAMA:	Alexander! Please try to remember this! It's very important! The bridge over the river has been weakened by the heavy rains - so stay away from the bridge!!
DUNKLE:	Alexander started on his walk and he really tried to remember.
ALEX:	Bridge is weak - the ridge is beek - the breek is widge - the crill is twine - the glurn is ploof an' <u>I forget!!!</u>
DUNKLE:	Just then, Hester the hyena, who was on her way to a party across the river, came by . . .
HESTER:	We're gonna play games, Alexander - but you can't remember any of the rules, so you weren't invited. I sorta wish you were, 'cause you're kinda cute - in a large way! We're gonna play tag, hide-and-seek, and pin-the-tail-on-the-hunter, and London Bridge is fallin' down, (SINGS) fallin' down, fallin' down (FADE) London Bridge is fallin' down . . .
ALEX:	Gee, games – with – with real friends, like – like I wish Hester was my friend! Tag, hide-and-seek, pin-the-tail-on-the–hunter an' . . . London Bridge (SINGS) is fallin' down, fallin' down - London Bridge . . .(UP) Bri . . .! Bridge!

	BRIDGE!! (CALLS) Hester! Stay off the bridge! Hester) Waaiiiit! (TRUMPETS)
DUNKLE:	Well, Alexander lumbered after her - extending his long trunk before him - Hester, halfway across the bridge by now, was lifted high in the air — Just in time, by bein' coiled in Alexander's trunk!! At first, she was very angry!
HESTER:	Stop that! Put me down!!
DUNKLE:	Then she was stunned as she watched the bridge crumple - and fall into the river, far, far below)
HESTER:	Oh, Alexander — you — you saved my life!!
ALEXANDER:	I did it! I finally remembered about the bridge - I finally learned to remember! (UP) Hester, uh, you could get on my back and I'd swim across the river . . . and then you wouldn't miss the swell party!
HESTER:	Party? What party? I'd much rather stay here with my new friend - and the hero who saved me!
ALEX:	But weren't you goin' to the party?
HESTER:	As you used to say, Alexander - I forget!
DUNKLE:	(LAFF) And that's how Alexander, the elephant, learned to remember because of his new friend — Hester!

"BECAUSE AUNT RAPUNZEL WAS THERE"

DUNKLE: Donnie, have you ever wondered about your Aunt Rapunzel and me?

DONNIE: Wondered about what?

DUNKLE: About how we got together . . . how we became an 'item.'

DONNIE: An 'item?' What's an 'item?'

DUNKLE: It means that people noticed that we were seeing a lot of each other . . . that we only went out with each other.

DONNIE: That's an 'item?'

DUNKLE: Yeah.

DONNIE: What about it?

DUNKLE: Well, I mean, have you ever wondered what the magic was that made Aunt Rapunzel and I discover we were both residents of the same planet - and that our coming together was dramatically realized by a series of possibly unrelated circumstances.

DONNIE: Huh?

DUNKLE: Did you ever wonder how Aunt Rapunzel and I got married?

DONNIE: Yeah . . . but every time you tell me it's different somehow. I thought you just met each other somewhere . . . like at school, maybe . . . and you liked each other . . . and like that.

DUNKLE: No, there was more to it than that. The very first time we set eyes on each other was at the top of Mount Everest. She was climbing up one side - and I was climbing up the other . . . and when I got to the top I looked across to the other side and I saw a pair of the most beautiful blue eyes I'd ever seen.

DONNIE: Aunt Rapunzel?

DUNKLE: No . . . her mule.

DONNIE: (UP) Her mule!!

DUNKLE: Yeah, the mule she was ridin' up to the top of Mount Everest.

DONNIE: You don't ride a mule to the top of Mount Everest!

DUNKLE: I know I didn't . . . but Aunt Rapunzel did.

DONNIE: That's not what I meant.

DUNKLE: It's what you said.

DONNIE: No, I said . . . or maybe I should have said . . . you 'can't' ride a mule to the top of Mount Everest.

DUNKLE: There's a law against it?

DONNIE: No, it's just impossible. There's too much snow and ice on the side of the mountain. The mule would slip and slide.

DUNKLE: Donnie, your knowledge of mules is sadly misunderstood. Mules are sure-footed and have no fear of heights.

DONNIE: Straight up?

DUNKLE: What do you mean . . . 'straight up?'

DONNIE: I mean that there aren't little roads going up the mountain. You have to climb straight up sometimes. You have to have hands to place those little hooks in the cracks . . . and pull yourself up. A mule couldn't do that.

DUNKLE: I don't want to go on and on about this. On second thought it was Aunt Rapunzel's beautiful blue eyes I saw.

DONNIE: . . . and there wasn't any mule?

DUNKLE: There wasn't any mule.

DONNIE: Then why did you say there was?

DUNKLE: I wanted to see if you'd believe it.

DONNIE: I didn't.

"Because Aunt Rapunzel Was There"   17

DUNKLE: So we dispense with the mule. Are you satisfied?

DONNIE: Just tell me what really happened. I'm a little confused.

DUNKLE: O.K. (PAUSE) As I said, I saw these beautiful blue eyes of Aunt Rapunzel - only I didn't know it <u>was</u> Aunt Rapunzel then - I just knew it was a beautiful blue mule . . .

DONNIE: . . . lady.

DUNKLE: . . . a beautiful blue-eyed lady mule.

DONNIE: No, just a beautiful blue-eyed lady. You said there wasn't any mule. Remember?

DUNKLE: I remember. You got me sort of mixed up there. We both reached the top of Mount Everest at the same precise moment. So there wasn't any question as to who got to the top first. We both did. And besides, the photos that the newspaper men took proved that we did.

DONNIE: What newspaper men?

DUNKLE: The ones on top of Mount Everest. You didn't think we would have climbed that dumb mountain if we weren't gonna get some publicity! You certainly didn't think that!

DONNIE: No, I guess I didn't think that.

DUNKLE: Anyway, Aunt Rapunzel and I got to talking and I asked if I could see her again and she said that would be O.K. So after we slid down Mount Everest to get to the bottom, we exchanged addresses and phone numbers.

DONNIE: Did you see each other again?

DUNKLE: You bet. She called me up the next morning - about three or four times.

DONNIE: Why so many times?

DUNKLE: I didn't answer the phone - so she kept calling.

DONNIE: Why didn't you answer the phone?

DUNKLE: Well, I was eating these caramels that was one of the prizes I got for climbing Mount Everest and I got some stuck in my tooth.

DONNIE: So you couldn't talk on the phone?

DUNKLE: So I couldn't talk on the phone, right. But she was really crazy about me and kept calling. Finally I managed to swallow all of the caramel and I answered the phone and it was him . . .

DONNIE: Him? Don't you mean 'her?'

DUNKLE: No, 'him' . . . it was the trainer of the mule. He was mad because he didn't get in any of the shots the newspaper men took.

DONNIE: I thought there wasn't any mule. You said there wasn't any mule.

DUNKLE: That's what I tried to tell the trainer. Then the other phone rang and I put the trainer on hold and who do you think was calling on the other phone?

DONNIE: Aunt Rapunzel.

DUNKLE: Aunt Rapunzel!! Our romance started right there. I made a date to go swimming with her in the pool in front of the Taj Mahal. We got a nice sun-tan and I asked her what she was doing the next day and she said she wasn't doing anything . . . so I said how about getting married.

DONNIE: And what'd she say?

DUNKLE: She said 'I thought you'd never ask!'

DONNIE: Why'd she say that?

DUNKLE: Because I was eating the last caramel I had left from my Mount Everest climb and it was stuck in my tooth. When I finally swallowed it, I asked her. Took me a week and a half to swallow that darn caramel!! I was sick of caramels! . . . and I told that to Aunt Rapunzel . . . and she said she had something better for me - something I'd like. And. I did!

DONNIE: Mustard fudge.

DUNKLE: Right! Mustard fudge! So the next day we got married and that's the true story of how Aunt Rapunzel and I got together. Any questions?

DONNIE: Just one. What happened to the mule trainer?

DUNKLE: Don't ask me. He's probably still on hold!

"BIGELOW BEE AND THE HONEY FACTORY"

DONNIE: (COMING ON) Uncle Dunkle!

SOUND: A FEW STEPS, THEN A SLIGHT TRIP

DONNIE: Oops . . . Uncle Dunkle? Are ya home?

RAPUNZEL: (OFF) I'll be right there! (THINKS) Unless you're a salesman sellin' somethin' I don't want.

DONNIE: (GIGGLES)

RAPUNZEL: If you are, I'll stay out here until you go away. (PAUSE) Are you a salesman?

DONNIE: (GIGGLE) What kind of salesman, Aunt Rapunzel?

RAPUNZEL: A salesman who sells things. But I don't have any nephew salesman.

SOUND: OPENS SCREEN DOOR

RAPUNZEL: Well, my stars! It's Donnie, My little nephew Donnie! How's my favorite nephew?

DONNIE: I'm the only nephew you've got, Aunt Rapunzel.

RAPUNZEL: It's true. It's true as humble bees and dish towels! But you'd be my favorite nephew . . . even if I had two-and-a-half-dozen nephews.

DONNIE: I'll accept that . . . as Uncle Dunkle might say.

RAPUNZEL: Does he say that?

DONNIE: No . . . but he might. (GIGGLES)

RAPUNZEL: (LAFF) Come in, Donnie . . . come in . . . oh, and watch out for the broken second step on the porch.

DONNIE: It's too late, Aunt Rapunzel. My little legs already took a trip.

RAPUNZEL: Oh . . . didn't you see the broken step?

DONNIE: I saw it . . . but my 'legs' didn't.

RAPUNZEL: I've asked your Uncle Dunkle to fix that step . . . but–

DONNIE: (DOWN) But, oh gee . . .

RAPUNZEL: Don't you worry yourself, Donnie . . . I'll tell you a story today!

DONNIE: (BRIGHT) Gee, Aunt Rapunzel, would ya? (CHANGE) Hey, wait a minute! How'd you know that's what I was thinkin' about?

RAPUNZEL: Well . . . when you first came in, you were wearing a smile that stretched from ear to ear and halfway 'round the back of your head!

DONNIE: Yeah?

RAPUNZEL: So now, dear, when I noticed your face was fallin' . . . I thought I'd better catch it before it hit the floor!

DONNIE: (GIGGLES)

RAPUNZEL: But before I begin my story . . . I thought we'd get better acquainted.

DONNIE: Aunt Rapunzel, I come over every day. How much more acquainted can we get?

RAPUNZEL: (IGNORING THAT) So . . . so how are you, Donnie?

DONNIE: Uncle Dunkle does his 'segue ways' much smoother.

RAPUNZEL: (CLEARS THROAT) Yes . . . well . . . uh, Uncle Dunkle was always better at . . . uh . . . that . . . (GOES ON) Now, Donnie . . .

DONNIE: Do you know what 'segue way' means?

RAPUNZEL: (FLUSTERED) Oh, of course, Donnie. Why, everyone knows that. (GOES ON) Now, Donnie . . . your uncle tells me . . .

DONNIE: What does it mean, Aunt Rapunzel?

RAPUNZEL: Segue way?

DONNIE: Segue way.

RAPUNZEL: It means . . . (BEAT) Segue way?

DONNIE: Segue way. What does it mean?

RAPUNZEL: It means . . .

DONNIE: Yes?

RAPUNZEL: It means . . .

DONNIE: Yes? Yes?

RAPUNZEL: (DOWN) I . . . I don't know.

DONNIE: (BRIGHT) That's O.K., Aunt Rapunzel - there's lot's of words that I don't know until you teach 'em to me . . . so this time I can teach you new word! A ' segue way' is some clever little word or sentence that Uncle Dunkle uses so he can 'slide with ease and grace' from one thought to another!

RAPUNZEL: Where did you ever learn that, Donnie?

DONNIE: From Uncle Dunkle . . . he's one smart cookie!

RAPUNZEL: Which brings me to my point . . . Your cookie . . . uh, I mean, uncle told me you need to wear glasses . . . (BEAT) for your 'eyes', I mean . . . not the 'iced tea' kind.

DONNIE: (MAD) Yeah. But I'm not gonna wear 'em.

RAPUNZEL: Why not?

DONNIE: 'cause glasses'll funny lookin'!!

RAPUNZEL: Oh, no they won't, dear. (BEAT) Your Uncle Dunkle wears glasses.

DONNIE: Like I said, they'll make me funny lookin'!

RAPUNZEL: Oh . . . Donnie!

DONNIE: (GIGGLES) Just kiddin' . . .

RAPUNZEL: I certainly hope so, dear . . . after all, he may be your 'smart cookie' uncle . . . but he's also the 'crumb' that I love!

DONNIE: (GIGGLES) Well, he's not funny lookin' . . . but I'll be funny lookin'!

RAPUNZEL: We'll see. (BEAT) Ready for your story?

DONNIE: Sure.

RAPUNZEL: It's all about glasses!

DONNIE: (UP) I knew you were leadin' up to this! (CHANGE). Uncle Dunkle would have been much smoother.

RAPUNZEL: With his 'segue ways'?

DONNIE: Right.

RAPUNZEL: Uncle Dunkle's not here, dear.

DONNIE: I know . . . he's buildin' a snowman in July.

RAPUNZEL: . . . massive . . .

DONNIE: Oh, yeah.

RAPUNZEL: (CLEARS THROAT) Donnie, do you know where honey comes from?

DONNIE: Is this another segue way?

RAPUNZEL: Uh, yes . . . it is.

DONNIE: Uncle Dunkle's a lot . . .

RAPUNZEL: . . . smoother. I know. (CHANGE) Anyway . . . do you know where honey comes from?

DONNIE: (DOWN) O.K., I'll go along with ya on this one . . . 'cause you're a good egg, Aunt Rapunzel!

RAPUNZEL: Is that like a smart cookie?

DONNIE: (GIGGLES) Close enough! (BEAT) Go on . . . ask me again!

RAPUNZEL: (STIFF) Gee . . . Donnie . . . do . . . you . . . know . . . where . . . honey . . . comes . . . from?

DONNIE: (STIFF) Why . . . no . . . Aunt . . . Rapunzel . . . I . . . don't.

RAPUNZEL: (NORMAL) I didn't either until Uncle Dunkle bought me a beehive.

DONNIE: What for?

RAPUNZEL: For my birthday.

DONNIE: That's a silly birthday present!

RAPUNZEL: Well, that's what he bought me . . .

DONNIE: It's still silly.

RAPUNZEL: . . . so I became a beekeeper - and everyday I went out to the beehive, wearing my special beekeeper suit and hat . . .

DONNIE: Why?

RAPUNZEL: So the bees wouldn't sting me.

DONNIE: Were the bees wearing suits and hats too?

RAPUNZEL: No, because they knew I didn't know how to sting themselves. (GOES ON) The beehive was like a busy little honey factory. There were very proud bees guarding the entrance of the hive. They were also very serious. I told them a joke and they didn't even crack a smile.

DONNIE: Do bees smile, Aunt Rapunzel?

RAPUNZEL: Well, I really couldn't tell if they smiled or not . . . bees don't have any teeth! (BEAT) Many of the bees were workers who collected nectar from the nearby flowers. Others worked inside the hive turning the nectar into sweet, sweet honey!

DONNIE: Sounds yummy!

RAPUNZEL: . . . and the entire job was overseen by the queen bee. (CHANGE) One day, I went out to the hive . . . and do you know what I heard?

DONNIE: No . . . what?

RAPUNZEL: I heard . . .

QUEEN BEE: Bigelow! Bigelow Bee!

BIGELOW: Yes, Queenie.

QUEEN: Don't be playful with me, Bigelow!

BIGELOW: Yes, Queenie . . . I mean . . . your Royal Highness.

QUEEN: Bigelow! Step into my office.

BIGELOW: Yes, your Royal Highness.

RAPUNZEL: But as poor little Bigelow stepped into the queen's office, he tripped.

BIGELOW: Whooooops!

SOUND: CRASH

QUEEN: Now I know why they call you a bumble bee!!

BIGELOW: 'Cause . . . I . . . bumble?

QUEEN: Correct.

SOUND: PAPER NOISE

QUEEN: According to this report, you have fallen behind in your work!

BIGELOW: How do you know that report is accurate?

QUEEN: Because . . . I wrote it myself!

BIGELOW: Oh.

QUEEN: According to this highly accurate report . . . which I wrote myself . . . all the other worker-bees are bringing in three times as much nectar as you.

BIGELOW: I'm tryin' as hard as I can. (SIGH)

QUEEN: Well . . . try harder . . . or . . . I'll have to fire you!

BIGELOW: F-f-fire me? (GULP) You mean I wouldn't get any more free honey samples?

QUEEN: Correct.

BIGELOW: I'd have to turn in my key to the washroom?

QUEEN: Correct.

BIGELOW: No more retirement plan?

QUEEN: Correct.

BIGELOW: I'll try harder.

QUEEN: Good. I'm glad we had this tiny chat, Bigelow.

BIGELOW: I'm glad, too, Queenie . . . I mean, your Royal Queenie . . . I mean, your Highly Queenship . . . I mean . . . oh, skip it.

QUEEN: . . . and I do hope you won't let me down.

BIGELOW: I won't . . . I won't!

QUEEN: . . . and you won't forget our little chat.

BIGELOW: I won't! I won't!

QUEEN: . . . and you'll bring in lots and lots of nectar.

BIGELOW: I won't . . . I won't . . .

QUEEN: What!!?

BIGELOW: I mean, I will! I will!

RAPUNZEL: And with that Bigelow bumbled out of the hive.

BIGELOW: Whooooops!

SOUND: CRASH

BIGELOW: (RECOVERS) I have to remember to watch that step! (BEAT) Now, I'll just fly right over to the big flower gar-

	den and bring back all the nectar my little stinger can carry! That's what I'll do!
DONNIE:	Did Bigelow do that, Aunt Rapunzel?
RAPUNZEL:	No, he didn't! Bigelow flew right past the flower garden! He didn't even notice it! . . . so I followed Bigelow.
DONNIE:	And where did he go?
RAPUNZEL:	He flew through an open window inside my house.
DONNIE:	It's Uncle Dunkle's house too!
RAPUNZEL:	Well, you know what I mean.
DONNIE:	Just keepin' ya on your toes! (BEAT) Did you follow Bigelow inside?
RAPUNZEL:	I surely did . . . and Bigelow was buzzing all over the house . . . going every which way . . . looking quite lost!
BIGELOW;	I sure have been flyin' for the ever-so-longest time. That big flower bed seems ever-so-much farther than it used to! (UP) Oh, wait a minute! There's a flower! A great big yellow flower! I see it! I see it now!!
RAPUNZEL:	But it wasn't a flower at all! Guess what Bigelow was lookin' at?
DONNIE:	I give up. What'?
RAPUNZEL:	It was a painting of a big yellow sunflower, hangin' on the wall. Well, Bigelow picked up speed . . .
SOUND:	LIGHT BUZZING

RAPUNZEL: . . . and with all his might . . . crashed, smack-dab, right into that painting!

SOUND: CRASH

BIGELOW: Ouch! That was ever-so-hard . . . for a flower, that is! Oooh, and I've done it now! I've bent my poor little stinger! Now I'll have to make a pit stop at the hive to get it fixed.

RAPUNZEL: So Bigelow Bee turned his bent little stinger around and headed for what he thought was the hive.

DONNIE: Wasn't it?

RAPUNZEL: No, it wasn't!

DONNIE: Ut-oh!

RAPUNZEL: Ut-oh, indeed! He was flying right towards . . . me! Bigelow flew straight into the bonnet I had on to keep me from getting stung.

BIGELOW: Say, the hive is . . . empty! All the bees are gone!

RAPUNZEL: Just then, Uncle Dunkle walked into the room . . .

DUNKLE: Rapunzel, dear?

RAPUNZEL: Yes, D'Artanyan?

DUNKLE: I don't know quite how to break this to ya . . . but you have a bee in your bonnet!

RAPUNZEL: I am well aware of that fact, D'Artanyan.

DUNKLE: Well, as long as you know about it . . . I mean, heck, if

"Bigelow Bee and the Honey Factory"   31

you want to go around wearin' a bee in your bonnet, I'm not going to stop ya. (TO HIMSELF) Crazy new styles! Whatever happened to just plain everyday hats? (GOING OFF) A bee in her bonnet . . . craziest thing I ever did see!

RAPUNZEL: . . . and Uncle Dunkle left me and the bee . . .

DONNIE: Did Uncle Dunkle come back?

RAPUNZEL: No, Donnie - he only had a small part in this story,

DONNIE: I'll accept that.

RAPUNZEL: As Uncle Dunkle might'd have said . . .

DONNIE: Yeah, if he had a bigger part!

RAPUNZEL: Well, after Uncle Dunkle left, I pleaded: Mr. Bee! Come out! It's me! Rapunzel, your honey-lovin' beekeeper! You're in my hat!

BIGELOW: In your hat? Sorry about that!

DONNIE: Did Bigelow fly out of your hat, Aunt Rapunzel?

RAPUNZEL: Yes . . . (SIGH) thank goodness . . . and I told him that I'd been following him all afternoon.

BIGELOW: Are you a spy for the queen?

RAPUNZEL: No, no . . . (LAFF) But I think I've solved your problem.

BIGELOW: My 'problem' is that I'm a bumbling bee! (BEGINS TO CRY)

RAPUNZEL: But only because you can't see!

BIGELOW: I can see! I can see! (BEAT) But . . . not very well, I'll admit.

RAPUNZEL: You mean, everything you see is fuzzy?

BIGELOW: (UP) Not all the time! Sometimes, if I squint hard, things are only blurry!

RAPUNZEL: Didn't you ever wonder why?

BIGELOW: No, ma'am - I just thought all bees saw things fuzzy . . . squinty . . . blurry . . .

RAPUNZEL: You couldn't find the big flower garden because you couldn't see where it was! You thought my bonnet was a bouquet! (LAFF) (CHANGE) You need to wear glasses.

BIGELOW: That's silly! Bees don't wear glasses!

RAPUNZEL: Well, then . . . you'll be the first! (BEAT) I'm taking you to Uncle Dunkle's eye doctor.

BIGELOW: Before we go . . . I have to fly back to the hive-hospital and get my poor little stinger unbent. Ouch! Only I don't know which way the hive-hospital is!

RAPUNZEL: So I pointed Bigelow Bee back toward the hive-hospital. Inside, a group of workers (who specialized in that sort of thing) straightened out his stinger. Next, I drove Bigelow to Uncle Dunkle's eye doctor. He checked out Bigelow's eyes and tested his vision.

DOCTOR: Yes, it's true, Bigelow. You will have to wear glasses. There's only one problem . . .

BIGELOW: You mean the money? Don't worry . . . the queen'll spring for it!!

DOCTOR: No, no . . . your problem is . . . you have no ears! How can we get the glasses to stay on you head?

BIGELOW: (THINKS HARD) I have two antennas!

DOCTOR; Why, so you do! Yes, we can attach your glasses to those.

RAPUNZEL: So the doctor had his good friend, the eye-glass-maker, fashion a special pair of tiny wire-framed glasses that fit just right on Bigelow's head . . . and attached perfectly to his antennas.

DONNIE: Was he funny lookin'?

RAPUNZEL: Not in the least! He was as handsome as handsome could be . . . in his glasses.

DONNIE: Gosh!

RAPUNZEL: Newspaper reporters came from far and near to interview the handsome little bee - the first to ever wear glasses.

REPORTER: Get a shot of that handsome little bee, Charlie! He looks great in those glasses!

CHARLIE: Smile, Mr. Bee. You're going to be famous!

RAPUNZEL: Bigelow gave a big smile. The man snapped the picture . . . and it appeared on the front page of every newspaper, with the headline: BEE   WEARS   GLASSES! (CHANGE) Now that Bigelow Bee could see, he became a top worker at the beehive honey factory. Very soon after, the Queen Bee once again invited him into her office. Only this time things went a bit differently . . .

QUEEN: Bigelow, you've brought in more honey than any other worker! Congratulations! You've changed!

BIGELOW: Thanks, Queenie!

QUEEN: (DOWN) You haven't changed that much! The rules haven't changed!! (UP) You don't call the queen, 'Queenie'!

BIGELOW: Sorry 'bout that. (BEAT) What should I call you?

QUEEN: Call me . . . 'partner'!

BIGELOW: Partner'?

QUEEN: Sounds good already! (BEAT) Yes, it's gonna be me and you, Bigelow Bee! See?

BIGELOW: I see! I see!

QUEEN: Those glasses must be working. (BEAT) You've done so well that we're expanding our hive! You're going to be the world's first . . . King Bee!

BIGELOW: Terrific!! (DOWN) . . . only . . .

QUEEN: Only what?

BIGELOW: I never heard of a King Bee.

QUEEN: Of course you haven't! Not until this very minute! I just made it up!! (LAFF)

RAPUNZEL: So Bigelow was a huge success! His glasses allowed him to see clearly . . . and even though he was now a big time executive, he still enjoyed the simple pleasures . . . and, from time to time, I still see him flying amongst the pretty flowers in my garden.

BIGELOW: Gee . . . the flowers are pretty! I would never have noticed that . . . if it weren't for my glasses!

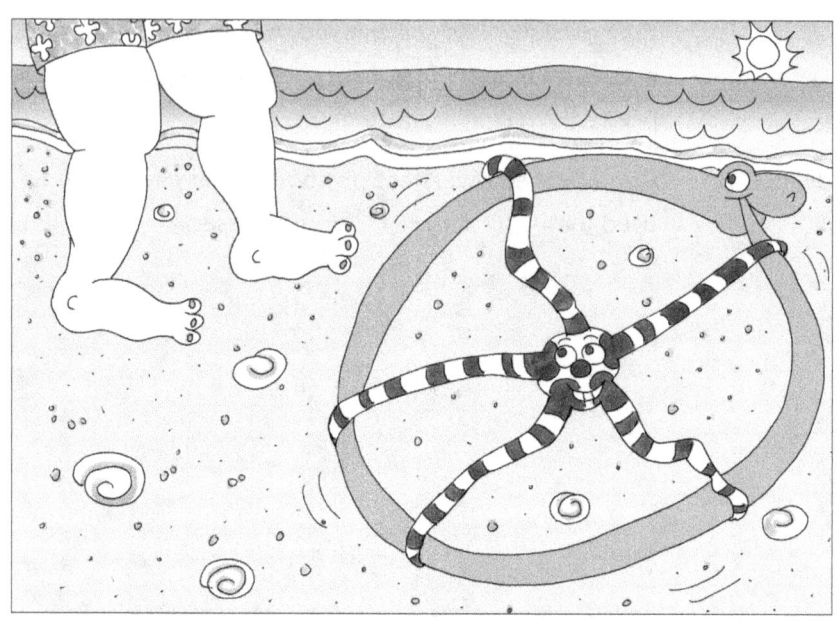

"BRITTY THE STARFISH"

DUNKLE: Donnie, mark this day down in your calendar as a day that's different from all other days - a day to remember. Today, I'm gonna tell you somethin' that'll be hard to believe . . .!

DONNIE: You tell me lots of things that're hard to believe.

DUNKLE: Yeah, but this will be even harder to believe!

DONNIE: What's this hard-to-believe story all about, Uncle Dunkle?

DUNKLE: It's about . . . a starfish! - but that's not what's hard to believe!

DONNIE: What is hard to believe?

"Britty the Starfish" 37

DUNKLE: The thing that's hard to believe . . . is that the kind of starfish I'm talkin' about breaks all to pieces when somebody tries to pick it up!!

DONNIE: It . . . it what?

DUNKLE: Breaks all to pieces! Everythin' jus' goes every which-way! The legs, or as they are technically known, the 'rays' of the star-fish fall off, and break all to smithereens!! All to pieces!

DONNIE: Then does the starfish . . . die?

DUNKLE: Oh, no - no, no, no, no! He jus' grows new legs - or rays. (QUICKLY) Takes time to bring this off, but he does it. (CHANGE) But what if he was goin' on a picnic or had an appointment to have his teeth cleaned by the dentist - he'd have to cancel it, and . . .

DONNIE: (UP) Uncle Dunkle!!

DUNKLE: Yeah?

DONNIE: I have a question - do starfish have teeth?

DUNKLE: Uh . . . no.

DONNIE: Do starfish have dentists?

DUNKLE: No.

DONNIE: But you said . . .

DUNKLE: (LAFF) I jus' wanted to see if you was payin' attention! Well, this kind of starfish is called a "Brittle Star" and the particular one I'm gonna tell you about - his name was Britty. Nice-lookin' . . . uh . . . for a starfish.

DONNIE: Pretty Britty!!

DUNKLE: No, not pretty - 'handsome' is the better word - but I am stretchin' the truth a little there – anyway, Britty liked nothin' better'n lyin' on the beach . . . jus' soakin' up the sun.

DONNIE: Sounds like Britty had it made!

DUNKLE: Well, maybe - only trouble was, that boys and girls wanted to pick him up and take him home . . . for a souvenir, or a pet! But little Britty, knowin' what his 'secret weapon' was, would wait until one of the kids reached down to get him and then ZINGO!! Britty would break all to pieces! Then, after the kids had left, Britty would start the slow process of growin' new legs . . .

DONNIE: . . . or 'rays', like you said.

DUNKLE: Yeah, rays – and he'd call up the dentist to cancel . . .

DONNIE: Ah, ah, ah! Uncle Dunkle!!

DUNKLE: (CHUCKLE) Oh yeah! He decided that he didn't have a dentist . . . sorry about that!

DONNIE: Uncle Dunkle, if Britty was so afraid of bein' caught, why didn't he jus' stay in the ocean where he was . . . safe?

DUNKLE: Ah, that's a good point, Donnie - but Britty was curious. He wanted to see what went on outside the great, incredibly large ocean he called home. He jus' couldn't resist lyin' on that beach. It was on the beach, y'know, that he met Slither.

DONNIE: I didn't know that!

DUNKLE: Yep, he met Slither.

"Britty the Starfish" 39

DONNIE: Slither?

DUNKLE: Yeah, that was his name - Slither. Slither was a snake - little ole field snake.

DONNIE: Uncle Dunkle, how comes it a field snake would crawl all the way down to the beach?

DUNKLE: That was 'cause Slither was a curious little feller, too. He always wondered what the ocean was like - not bein' a swimmin' type snake, y'see . . .

DONNIE: I see.

DUNKLE: Slither and Britty were both on the beach this day - not payin' any attention to each other fer quite a spell - and then Slither - well, he shook himself and sorta sighed. Then he started talkin' to himself . . .

SLITHER: Sure would like to know what it's like down there at the bottom of the ocean. Wonder if the folks that run the ocean put out a free booklet I could send away for - explainin' about it.

BRITTY: I can tell you about it, Mr . . . uh . . .

SLITHER: Will you tell me about it for free? If you won't, I could probably get a free booklet tellin' about it . . .

BRITTY: I'll tell about it free!

SLITHER: Ah, first rate! My name's Slither!

BRITTY: You're a snake . . .

SLITHER: How can you tell?

BRITTY: Well . . . uh . . . you don't look much like a French poodle!

SLITHER: How discerning you are! I am indeed a snake. What are you? I don't mean to be rude!

BRITTY: I'm a brittle starfish - name's Britty.

SLITHER: Well . . . tell me.

BRITTY: Tell you what?

SLITHER: About the ocean - you said you would.

BRITTY: Well . . . it's big and wet and . . . down deep . . . it's dark.

SLITHER: Ah, that's beautiful - you're a regular poet. What a way with words you have!!

BRITTY: Slither . . . uh . . . what's it like out there . . . y'know, in the fields where you come from?

SLITHER: Ah, yes! The fields!! Well, there are these flowers - they call them sunflowers - they grow on a long stem - very pretty.

BRITTY: I got me a starfish cousin sounds like that!

SLITHER: Like the sunflower?

BRITTY: Yeah, my cousin is called a "Rosy-Feather Starfish" - grows on the end of a long stem, too - lots of tiny joints fastened together . . . and when he gets older, he'll break himself free and just swim away . . .

DUNKLE: Well, sir, Donnie - Britty and Slither became good friends - each one tellin' the other about a world he'd never seen . . . Britty describin' the creatures of the sea - and Slither, the farm animals and . . . wagons . . . and things. One day, some boys and girls came down to the beach. They thought catchin' a brittle starfish would be great sport.

BRITTY:	Oh, Slither! Dear friend, Slither! These are the boys and girls I was tellin' you about! They want to catch me and take me away from the beach. I could go all to pieces like I usually do - but then I'd have to grow new rays . . .
SLITHER:	. . . and maybe have to cancel a dental appointment! Cool it, cool it, kid! I got an idea for savin' ya!! Do you remember I was tellin' you about wagons? And wagon wheels?
BRITTY:	Hurry! Hurry! Hurry!
SLITHER:	You and me, Britty - we're gonna be . . . a wheel!
DUNKLE:	And here's how they did it, Donnie — Slither wrapped himself around the five legs or rays of Britty, makin' a circle, get the picture?
DONNIE:	Uh-huh.
DUNKLE:	Then he grabbed the end of his tail in his mouth, contracted all his muscles - and lifted Britty to an upright position - and then, jus' like a regular wheel, Slither and Britty started rollin' down the beach - faster'n'faster they went, leavin' the boys and girls far behind. They didn't catch Britty then . . . or ever again. With his pal, Slither, around, Britty knew they could stay on the beach, talkin' in peace - with no fear of his ever bein' caught. Yessir, Slither and Britty were some pair!!
DONNIE:	They're what you'd call . . . a "big wheel" - right, Uncle Dunkle?
DUNKLE:	(LAFF) They sure were!!

"DONNIE AND THE PIGGY BANK"

DUNKLE: Now, this time I'm gonna tell you about a particularly interestin' dream that Donnie had the other night. Donnie told me about it and I thought maybe you'd like to hear about it. Y'See, I had to go to the city the other day and by the time I'd returned, it was too late to tell a bedtime story to Donnie, because he was just about asleep. He'd tried to stay awake, but couldn't quite make it. I said:

DUNKLE: Donnie! Donnie boy! It's Uncle Dunkle! I've got a present for you!

DONNIE:	(SLEEPY) Hi, Uncle Dunkle. I'm almost asleep. (UP) Did you say you had a present for me?
DUNKLE:	I sure did! Open your eyes and take a look! Not enough to wake up . . . just enough to see what I brought you!
DONNIE:	(SLEEPY-INTERESTED) It's a piggy-bank - a great, big, pink piggy-bank!
DUNKLE:	You like it, Donnie? Look here, it's all made out of tin.
DONNIE:	Uh-huh - Gosh, I'll never, ever get enough pennies to fill it - it's so big!! So very very big . . . (FADING) Golly, I just can't seem to stay awake . . .!!
SOUND:	HIT CYMBAL WITH BRUSH
DONNIE:	(FADE IN) (YAWN) Where am I? Why . . . I'm . . . I'm on an island! And look, there's all kinds of fruit trees, orange, date, banana, coconut, pineapple, papaya - and there's even a little freshwater spring!! I don't know where I am, but at least I won't get hungry or thirsty. I wonder (UP) Oh, my goodness!! What's that over there? It's a big, pink, piggy-bank!!!
PIGGY:	Oink, oink! Hello, Donnie – my name is Pinky.
DONNIE:	Hiya, Pinky!
PIGGY:	I'd say 'welcome' - but I really think this is terrible place to be!
DONNIE:	Terrible? I admit, I'd like it much better if Uncle Dunkle was here, but at least there's fruit and water.
PIGGY:	Fruit and water mean nothing to me.

DONNIE: What do you eat, piggy-bank?

PIGGY: Money! I eat money! What I wouldn't give right now for some nice, juicy pennies - or a great big, luscious five-dollar bill, smothered in dimes - yum-yum - but look around. There's nothin' for this old piggy-bank to eat!!

GULL: (SQUAWK) Here, here, Pinky! Don't you go feelin' sorry for yerself!!

DONNIE: Who . . . who said that?

GULL: I did. I'm a seagull. Yessir, and I'm an old-timer in these parts - flown the seven seas, man and boy, for twenty years, and I'll show you where there's somethin' fer you to eat, Pinky!!

PIGGY: Where? Where? I'm starved!!

GULL: Right over . . . there! (BEAT) See what I see?

DONNIE: I see it. It's an old treasure-chest - just like Cap'n Kidd had! Let's look inside . . .

SOUND: PRY LID OFF – SQUEAKY

Oh, wow! Look, Pinky - you're really in luck!

GULL: See all those coins? They're called 'pieces of eight!'

PIGGY: Eight, huh? Well, it's about time I 'ate' my breakfast, so I'll just eat some of these pieces of eight!!

SOUND: EATING COINS – THROUGHOUT THE FOLLOWING SCENE

DONNIE: . . . and while you're eating, I'll have some fruit. Will you join me, Mr. Gull?

GULL: Don't mind if I do, Donnie.

DONNIE: Hey, Pinky, don't stuff yourself - you'll get sick! Oh, he's eating so fast - he's not listening, Mr . . . uh . . . Mr . . . (UP) Do you have a name, Mr. Gull?

GULL: A name? Come to think of it - no.

DONNIE: Well, let's see - you're a seagull . . .

GULL: Uh-yeah!

DONNIE: . . .and you travel . . .

GULL: Man and boy, I've flown the seven seas for . . .

DONNIE: . . .twenty years, I know!! Hmm (UP) Hey . . . Gull - travel - I've got a name for you! Your name's Gulliver - like in Gulliver's Travels!!!

GULL: Gulliver! Hey, I like that!!

DONNIE: It's O.K., Gulliver, glad to do it! (PAUSE) Say, Pinky, are you still eatin'? Haven't you had enough coins yet? You're eatin' too much — you better stop!! I mean it — don't eat anymore! Stop, Pinky, stop!!!

SOUND: METAL BREAKING

PIGGY: Oh dear, I ate so much, I broke in two!! I split right down the middle of my back!

DONNIE: You just stuffed yourself too much, that's all! What'll I do, Gulliver? I haven't anything to put him back together with. Uncle Dunkle has a soldering-iron. Uncle Dunkle could put him back together with that, but we're way out here

	. . . and he's way over on the mainland, wherever that is, and we can't get back there 'cause we haven't got a boat!!
GULL:	Sure ya have! You've got two boats!!
DONNIE:	Two boats?
GULL:	Each half of Pinky will float in the water like a boat - and if you make yourself a paddle, you can get inside and paddle your way to the mainland!
PIGGY:	Wait a minute! You can't leave the other half of me here!!
DONNIE:	I know what we'll do! I'll tie the other half of you to the one I'll use for a boat - and it'll just kinda trail along behind us.
GULL:	And I'll fly ahead to guide you. You just keep your eye on me and we'll get Pinky back to the mainland in a jiffy!!
DONNIE:	O.K. - I've got Pinky tied together. Here's a stick I use for a paddle . . .
GULL:	. . . and we're all ready to get under way!!!
DONNIE:	Let's go!!!
SOUND:	HIT CYMBAL WITH BRUSH
DONNIE:	(FADE IN) . . . and, of course, when I woke up, Pinky was there on the bed beside me and I was very happy - 'cause he wasn't broken at all - and it would have been awful if he was, 'cause I just remembered that your soldering-iron was broken . . . and you couldn't have put Pinky back together again and that would have been terrible 'cause . . .!!!!
DUNKLE:	(LAFF) But, Donnie, you're forgettin' — like I told you before, it was all a dream . . .

"DUNKLE'S OLD JALOPY"

DONNIE: Say . . . Uncle Dunkle?

DUNKLE: Yes, Donnie?

DONNIE: What happened to your old 'jalopy'?

DUNKLE: You mean my 'car'?

DONNIE: Well . . . yeah. (BEAT) I jus' call it a 'jalopy' . . . 'cause it's . . . well . . . kinda 'old' . . .

DUNKLE: It's <u>very</u> old.

DONNIE: I know. I was jus' tryin' to spare your feelings . . . 'cause I know how much you 'love' your old jalopy - I mean, 'car' . . .

DUNKLE: Yes . . . my ol' jalop—uh, car . . . is my pride'n' joy!

DONNIE: I know! You're always polishin' it . . .

DUNKLE: . . . to keep his gray lil body-a-shinin'!

DONNIE: His body?

DUNKLE: Sure! My car's got a name!

DONNIE: Uh-huh. (CAUTIOUS) What's his name, Uncle Dunkle?

DUNKLE: Stanley . . . Stanley the Steamer!

DONNIE: How do ya know?

DUNKLE: 'cause he told me.

DONNIE: Your jalopy did.

DUNKLE: No, my 'car' did.

DONNIE: Whatever. (BEAT) Uncle Dunkle?

DUNKLE: Yes, Donnie?

DONNIE: I didn't know 'cars' could talk.

DUNKLE: Well . . . ya see, Donnie . . . it's a special language . . . a language of admiration and friendship . . . that can only be understood by an owner and his prize vehicle.

DONNIE: But . . . Uncle Dunkle . . . my bike never talks to me . . .

DUNKLE: That'd be downright silly! Bicycles can't talk!

DONNIE: But, Uncle Dunkle . . .

DUNKLE: Donnie, when you get to be my age, you'll understand these things.

DONNIE: I guess you're right.

DUNKLE: 'course I am. (CHANGE) My car and I have a unique bond . . . and a long history together. I purchased Stanley about the time I was courtin' your Aunt Rapunzel . . .

DONNIE: That's swell . . . but . . .

DUNKLE: . . . and Stanley was old even then! He was built long before automobiles ran on gasoline! He runs on . . . steam!

DONNIE: But . . .

DUNKLE: 'Stanley the Steamer.'

DONNIE: But . . . But . . .

DUNKLE: (COY) I sure would be heartbroken if anything were to happen to my good old Stanley.

DONNIE: But . . . But . . . But . . . But . . .

DUNKLE: Donnie? What's the matter? You sound jus' like Stanley tryin' to start on a chilly mornin' . . . (CHANGE) Say, why all this fuss about my car, anyway?

DONNIE: I've been tryin' t'tell ya! Your old 'jalopy' . . .

DUNKLE: Car.

DONNIE: Your 'car' is . . . <u>gone</u>! It's not parked outside!

DUNKLE: (LAFF)

DONNIE: I don't think it's very funny.

DUNKLE: (LAFF) It's kinda funny.

DONNIE: I don't think it's funny at all.

DUNKLE (LAFF)

DONNIE: Uncle Dunkle?

DUNKLE: (LAFF)

DONNIE: (INSISTENT) Uncle Dunkle?

DUNKLE: (LAFF) Yes, Donnie?

DONNIE: Why are ya laughin'?

DUNKLE: Because you, Donnie . . . without even knowin' it . . . you have lead me to the topic of today's story.

DONNIE: Oh! I get it now! This is goin' to be the story of what happened to your old . . . uh, car

DUNKLE: No. My old 'jalopy.'

DONNIE: Huh? (BEAT) You've been puttin' me on, haven't ya?

DUNKLE: Well, someone's got to do it . . . might as well be me! (LAFF)

DONNIE: (GIGGLES)

DUNKLE: Now, Donnie . . . The whole thing began one day last week. I was out in the garage, conversin' with ol' Stanley when he up and said:

STANLEY: Sakes, D'Artanyan, all this conversin' has made me plumb hungry.

DUNKLE: What's your pleasure, Stanley? Oil? Gasoline? Peanut Brittle? Pizza? How 'bout some of Aunt Rapunzel's mustard custard?

STANLEY: (TEMPTED) The mustard custard sure sounds appetizin'

"Dunkle's Old Jalopy"   51

... but (UP) sakes, you know I can only drink <u>water</u>! I'm on a diet . . . gotta watch my 'intake' . . . I'm gettin' a <u>spare tire</u>!

DUNKLE: O.K., O.K., don't get 'steamed,' Stanley . . . here's your water . . .

SOUND: WATER BEING POURED

STANLEY: Glug! Glug! Glug! Glug! (SWALLOWS)

SOUND: WATER IS STILL POURED

STANLEY: Glug! Glug! (SWALLOWS) Hey! Glug! Glug! Hold on there, sonny! Glug! Glug! (SWALLOWS) Glug! Glug! Glug!

SOUND: WATER IS STILL POURED – THEN STOPS

DUNKLE: Have ya had enough water, Stanley?

STANLEY: Had enough?! Why, I'm plumb over-flowin' . . . (SMILES) with 'contentment, that is! Thanks!

DUNKLE: Glad to do it!

STANLEY: And now that you've fed me, D'Artanyan - where would ya like to go? Just name the spot and I'll be mighty happy to take ya there.

DUNKLE: . . . uh, let's see . . . (UP) oh, I know - Aunt Rapunzel wanted me to do the grocery shoppin' today. You can take me to the supermarket.

STANLEY: Supermarket? (MAD) Sakes, I was hopin' you'd wanna go someplace excitin'! We never have any adventures!

DUNKLE: What'd ya have in mind?

STANLEY: A drive across the Mojave Desert! (LAFFS) Man, now that's excitin' . . . by horny-toad! (LAFFS)

DUNKLE: Too hot for me.

STANLEY: How 'bout a drive along the rocky cliffs of the Pacific Ocean? That oughta cool your gizzards!

DUNKLE: I . . . think I'll pass on it.

STANLEY: Well, for the love o' Pete - what do ya wanna do?

DUNKLE: Go to the supermarket.

STANLEY: By horny-toad! That's just about the most <u>unexciting</u> thing I ever heard of! (BEAT) I sure would rather have me an <u>adventure</u> . . . even us <u>old</u> automobiles gotta have some fun . . . but if you wanna go shoppin' I (YAWNS) guess . . . I'll . . . have to take ya there. (DISAPPOINTED) Hop in.

SOUND: MOTOR STARTING . . . THEN PUT-PUT THE STEAM ENGINE UNDER:

DUNKLE: (TO HIMSELF) Let's see . . . I have to buy . . . mustard for the custard and kumquats for the fudge . . . catchup for the cookies . . . sardines for the cupcakes . . . pickles for the ice cream . . .

STANLEY: (UP) Can't we go any faster? I'm a car, not a push-cart! Let's get the lead out! Step on <u>me</u>! . . . my pedal, that is!

DUNKLE: We're already doin' the speed limit!

STANLEY: You never let me do anythin' excitin'!!!

DUNKLE: But, Stanley . . .

STANLEY: If I could control my own pedal . . . (LAFFS) . . . then, you'd see how fast I could go! Vrooom! Vroom! Vroooooooom (COUGHS) I think I got a clog in my steam pipe! Got that 'cause you never let me go fast enough to clean 'er out!

DUNKLE: But . . .

STANLEY: Someday, I'll go as fast as I want!

DUNKLE: But . . . But . . .

STANLEY: And I'll have me an 'adventure'!

DUNKLE: But . . . But . . . But . . . But . . .

STANLEY: You sound just like I do when I try to start up on a cold mornin' . . .

DUNKLE: But . . . But . . . But . . . But . . .

STANLEY: Turn off your engine, sonny!

DUNKLE: Out here? In the middle of the road?

STANLEY: No, no . . . not <u>my</u> engine! By horny-toad! Spit out whatever you're tryin to say!

DUNKLE: I just think you're too old a car to wanna live your life in the fast lane.

STANLEY: Now, I am getting' 'steamed' . . . (BEAT) D'Artanyan, are you sayin' that <u>this ole gray car ain't what he used to be</u>?

DUNKLE: No, no . . .

STANLEY: I could <u>beat</u> any of those 'revved-up' sports jobs any day of the week!

DUNKLE: I know, I know . . .

STANLEY: I'm fit as a fiddle . . . and tuned as a tuba!

DUNKLE: I know . . . I . . . (UP) Oh, here's the supermarket . . .

SOUND: CAR PULLING OVER . . . ENGINE STOPS

DUNKLE: Well, Stanley, why don' ya take a lil 'snooze' . . . while I go shoppin'.

STANLEY: A 'snooze'? Sakes, whatta ya think I am?

DUNKLE: Well, it was a long drive . . . I thought maybe you were tired . . . that's all.

STANLEY: (LAFF) Guess my crank-case is kinda . . . well, cranky today. Sorry.

DUNKLE: You're forgiven. (BEAT) I'll be back shortly.

SOUND: CAR DOOR OPENS AND CLOSES

STANLEY: (CALLS) And D'Artanyan?

DUNKLE: (OFF) Yes?

STANLEY: While you're in there, bring me back some o' that bubbling French spring water. It's got a real 'kick' to it!

DUNKLE: So, Donnie, I went shoppin' . . . leavin' Stanley the Steamer alone in the parkin' lot – only I made a terrible mistake! Do you know what that was?

DONNIE: You left your wallet home?

DUNKLE: Worse than that.

"Dunkle's Old Jalopy"   55

DONNIE: What could be worse than leavin' your wallet home when you went shoppin'?

DUNKLE: I left the <u>key</u> in Stanley's starter!

DONNIE: Oh, no!

DUNKLE: Oh, yes . . .

DONNIE: Oh, no!

DUNKLE: Yes, I did!

DONNIE: I meant, "Oh, no!" . . . as in . . . 'That's terrible, Uncle Dunkle!'

DUNKLE: Oh, no . . .

DONNIE: Oh, yes! (GIGGLE)

DUNKLE: Yes, sir, I left the key in his starter . . . <u>and</u> I even forgot to lock his door!

DONNIE: That <u>is</u> worse, Uncle Dunkle! What happened?

DUNKLE: Well, Aunt Rapunzel had given me an extra-long shoppin' list - so I was in that supermarket for hours . . .

STANLEY: (SNORES) Huh? (WAKING UP) Oh . . . (STRETCHES) By horny-toad! I did doze off after all! (YAWNS) Sure hope nobody saw me . . . I got an image to protect! (BEAT) I musta slept for hours! Sakes! It's as dark as a freshly laid driveway! (THINKS) And where's D'Artanyan? Gosh, maybe he's angry wit' me . . . and he ain't a-comin' back! I was kinda nasty to him earlier. Guess I jus' got up on the wrong side o' the garage this mornin' . . . (WORRIED) Maybe he's plumb up and left me here . . . forever! (CHANGE - UP) Oh, sakes, here he comes now . . . (CALLS) D'Artanyan! I thought ya plumb up and forgot me! (PAUSE) D'Artanyan? Did ya get that there fancy French spring water? (PAUSE) D'Artan– (DOWN) That there ain't D'Artanyan . . . that there's a . . . a stranger steppin' out of the shadows! (GASP) And he's a comin' this way!

SOUND: CAR DOOR OPENS AND CLOSES

He got inside me!

SOUND: ENGINE STARTING AND REVVING

Sakes! You can't take me! I don't belong to ya! (DOWN) By hornytoad, he can't hear me! (UP) Hey, we're a movin'!

SOUND: ENGINE PUT-PUT GETTING FASTER AND FASTER

DONNIE: And what happened, Uncle Dunkle?

DUNKLE: Well, it turns out that the fellow drivin' Stanley was wanted by the police . . . for stealin' cars!

DONNIE: He stole poor old Stanley? (SAD) Gee, Uncle Dunkle, that's just about the most unhappy ending to a story that you ever told!

DUNKLE: But, wait, Donnie, there's more!

DONNIE: There is?! Whew! I'm sure am glad of that!

DUNKLE: Once the car-nabber really got moving - Stanley started to . . . well, kinda enjoy it. He had always wanted to feel what it was like to drive fast – feel the wind on his running boards - and now he had his chance.

DONNIE: And did he like it?

DUNKLE: Well, he did . . . at first. He was drivin' along at a good clip when all of a sudden he saw flashing red lights behind him — and heard the shrill sound of a siren!

SOUND: SIREN UP - PUT-PUT OF ENGINE UNDER:

STANLEY: By horny-toad, it's the police! It's about time - 'cause we were even goin' too fast for <u>me</u>!

DUNKLE: Except . . . instead of pullin' over when the police car started chasin' them . . . the car-nabber increased his speed! . . . and Stanley could do nothin' about it but keep on movin'! (PAUSE) The wild chase might've gone on for hours . . . days . . . if one thing hadn't have happened. (BEAT) Stanley wasn't much enjoyin' himself by this point — and when the driver took Stanley 'round a very sharp turn . . . Stanley got really scared! He closed his eyes, and when he did, his headlights went out just long enough for the driver to lose control! And Stanley was plunged right into a big lake!

DONNIE: Stanley drowned? Boy! That ending's even sadder!

DUNKLE: No, no! Donnie, there's more! The police came and 'fished' Stanley and the robber out of the lake . . .

DONNIE: Whew!

DUNKLE: . . . and then, do you know what happened?

DONNIE: Sure! Since the car robber was wanted by the police, old Stanley got a big, fat reward!

DUNKLE: Right! . . . and what else?

DONNIE: The robber was sent to jail!

DUNKLE: . . . and what else?

DONNIE: Stanley was happy - 'cause he finally had his 'adventure' - and he learned that drivin' fast ain't all it's cracked up to be!

DUNKLE: Right! (BEAT) Anything else?

DONNIE: . . . and we're havin' fish for dinner tonight!

DUNKLE: That's right, we are! But how'd you know that?

DONNIE: Easy. While your old gray jalopy was down on the bottom of the lake, he caught some trout — so his trip wouldn't be a total loss!

DUNKLE: You're a very bright boy.

DONNIE: I know.

DUNKLE: Hmm?

DONNIE: Nothin' . . . (THINKS) Say, Uncle Dunkle? If everything turned out all right for your old gray jalopy . . . then, where is he now?

DUNKLE: Oh, a policeman took him away.

DONNIE: (WORRIED) What for?

DUNKLE: To give him his reward . . . a new paint job! (CHUCKLE) He'll be back tomorrow.

DONNIE: Your old gray jalopy?

DUNKLE: No, Donnie . . . my old red jalopy.

"HELPFUL THE DWARF"

DUNKLE: Donnie?

DONNIE: Yeah?

DUNKLE: Did you help Aunt Rapunzel with the dishes tonight?

DONNIE: Uh-huh. (SIGHS) Jus' like always.

DUNKLE: Why the long face?

DONNIE: Well, I really don' much like washin' dishes, Uncle Dunkle. But I figger if it eases Aunt Rapunzel's workload . . . then . . . what the hey!

DUNKLE: What the hey, indeed!

DONNIE: Only . . .

DUNKLE: Only what?

DONNIE: She usually gives me a couple o' cookies for helpin' out.

DUNKLE: And tonight she didn't.

DONNIE: Nope.

DUNKLE: Maybe she didn't bake any.

DONNIE: I know she did - 'cause I took the liberty of helpin' her bake 'em . . . without bein' asked!

DUNKLE: Oh, well, you wouldn't've wanted any of those anyway.

DONNIE: Why not?

DUNKLE: 'cause those were catchup and onion cookies!

DONNIE: They were not!

DUNKLE: Well, they were some kinda cookies.

DONNIE: They were gingerbread cookies! My favorite!

DUNKLE: Well, anyway . . . (Were they really gingerbread cookies?) . . . Donnie, you can't expect . . . (I like gingerbread cookies a lot too!) . . . Donnie, you shouldn't . . . (Of course, I don' like 'em as much as you do, y'see.) . . . You shouldn't . . . (Or maybe I like 'em more than you . . . I dunno) . . . Anyway, the point is - it's not a good idea to expect a reward every time ya do somethin' nice fer someone. It's kinda like jumpin' in a lake an' expectin' the fishes to hold ya up! (CHANGE) I knew this magical dwarf once . . .

DONNIE: You knew a magical dwarf?

DUNKLE: Yup. Well, long time ago I did.

DONNIE: Did he like gingerbread cookies?

DUNKLE: I never asked. (CHANGE) Anyway, (Hmm, I wonder if he . . . uh, never mind!) . . . This dwarf's name was Helpful. Know why?

DONNIE: 'cause he was 'helpful'?

DUNKLE: Right. Who says yer dumb! Now, Donnie, ole Helpful lived in a small wooden cottage . . . in an enchanted forest . . . and . . .

DONNIE: Uncle Dunkle?

DUNKLE: Yes, Donnie?

DONNIE: Who says I'm dumb?

DUNKLE: Nobody.

DONNIE: Then, why did ya, say it?

DUNKLE: It's just a figger of speech . . . it means, "Boy, are you smart!"

DONNIE: I'll accept that.

DUNKLE: (GOES ON) Everyday, Helpful would get up at the crack o' dawn and work all day in the nearby diamond mine - ten, twelve hours sometimes . . .

DONNIE: Why'?

DUNKLE; 'cause he was all alone . . . and was doin' the work of seven or eight of his kind!

DONNIE: Didn't he have any help?

DUNKLE: Well, he had a whole mess o' brothers who could have helped. They owned the mine - but they lived far away in another enchanted forest . . .

DONNIE: There's more than one?

DUNKLE: Dozens. Hundreds!

DONNIE: I didn't know that!

DUNKLE: Well, you're young, Donnie, you're young! (BEAT) . . . and his brothers were all too lazy to make the trek over to help him with his minin' chores . . . and magical dwarf work laws weren't as strict as they are now! So poor Helpful mined those diamonds everyday while his brothers just sat back and reaped the rewards of his labors! Helpful really didn't mind minin' all by himself . . . but he did wish that someday his brothers would realize how hard he worked - and at least thank him . . . (CHANGE) Well, one day, there was a knock at Helpful's door.

SOUND: DOOR OPENS

DWARF #1: Hey, lil brother! How's it goin'? Long time . . . an' all that jazz!

HELPFUL: Who are you?

DWARF #1: Hey, man, like, I'm your brother, brother! You dig?

HELPFUL: Well, I 'dig' in the mines . . . if that's what you mean.

DWARF #1: No, no, man - we're related . . . like, 'I am you . . . an' you are me . . . an' we are altogether!!'

HELPFUL: I have not seen any of my brothers in many, many years.

DWARF #1: An', like, you forget me already! For shame, man . . . for shame!

HELPFUL: Well, I guess you're my brother . . . or else you wouldn't be here.

DWARF #1: Hey! Hard logic to fight, baby. Now, you don' mind if I, like, move in wit' ya, man! I gotta get away, man! Like, there's this evil Queen, who's after me . . . an' I need a real safe hide-out - you dig?

HELPFUL: Well, in the mines I do . . .

DWARF #1: So, like . . . can I 'move in' . . . 'clean up' . . . an' 'chow down'?

HELPFUL: Yes. You may stay.

DWARF #1: Thanks, man! You're a dwarf-an'-a-half!

DUNKLE: So Helpful's brother stayed! But, still, he did no work!! Poor Helpful mined all day . . . and when he got home at night, it was always the same!

DWARF #1: Hey, Helpful, man - why don' you like darn my socks for me while you're waitin' for that stew to brew!

DUNKLE: Or . . .

DWARF #1: Hey, Helpful, man - my bed ain't made, man! Like, how am I supposed to get my beauty rest, baby?

DUNKLE: Or . . .

DWARF #1: Hey, Helpful, man - when ya gonna dust these stairs? There's like enough 'dirt' on these things, man, to support plant life!

DUNKLE: . . . and all the while, Helpful just thought to himself:

HELPFUL: Someday he'll thank me!

DUNKLE: But he never did, Donnie . . . Well, one day, months later . . . another knock came at the door . . .

SOUND: DOOR OPENS

DWARF #2: Hey, lil brother! How's it goin'? Long time . . . an' all that jazz!

HELPFUL: Who are you?

DWARF #2: Hey, man, like, I'm your brother, brother! You dig?

HELPFUL: Well, I dig in the mines . . . if that's what you mean . . . (FADES)

DUNKLE: You guessed it! Another brother moved in with Helpful! Now, he had two freeloaders livin' with him! Things went just about the same . . . only double, of course. But worse was to come! Every few months, another brother would show up at Helpful's door step . . . begging to stay there . . . and hide from the mean ole Queen! Now, the situation was really bad - seven brothers all giving orders to one helpless . . . Helpful . . .

DWARF #1: Hey, Helpful, man - how's 'bout washin' my shirts, man!

DWARF #2: Hey, Helpful, man - where's my teeth-type brush, baby?

DWARF #3: Hey, Helpful, man - I sure am like gettin' hungry, you dig?

DWARF #4: Forget the food, man! I'm, like, real thirsty!

"Helpful the Dwarf"   65

DWARF #3:   Bring me the grub first, man!

DWARF #4:   After my drink, of course!

DWARF #5:   But what about darnin' my socks, man!

DWARF #6:   Forget them, Helpful, man! Give me a bath, baby!

DUNKLE: Well, Helpful went on like this - waitin' on his brothers for a time - but he soon became very tired . . . and one day, he sat down to rest in the diamond mine . . . and began to think:

HELPFUL: Why, do I help all my brothers . . . when they're only taking advantage of me? (BEAT) I was always taught to be kind to others and to do whatever I can to help them! But I'm tired! And none of them ever help out at all!

DUNKLE: Then, suddenly, he thought of the answer:

HELPFUL: Maybe . . . by doin' all their work for them, I haven't really been helping them at all! Yeah! If I really want to help my brothers, I should go away from here - and then, they will have to learn to work the diamond mine . . . or starve! I hope they choose working!

DUNKLE: So Helpful packed up his stuff and moved away . . . far, far away. Eventually, when their money started to get low, his seven brothers had no choice but to start workin' in the diamond mine. They soon figgered out that if they all worked at the same time - they wouldn't have to work as hard . . . and they could get more done . . . and faster to boot!

DONNIE: Boy, Helpful sure taught them a good lesson.

DUNKLE: He sure did, Donnie. However, with Helpful gone, they never cleaned the house . . . or themselves! They never ate properly . . . an' always had holes in their socks! Of course, eventually - they learned how to be clean and healthy, too!

DONNIE: Who taught them that, Uncle Dunkle?

DUNKLE: Well, you see, Donnie, about a week after Helpful left . . . a beautiful, young girl . . . moved in with the seven dwarfs. Her name? . . . was Snow White!!

"HUMPTY-DUMPTY'S FRIEND"

DUNKLE: Say, Donnie, I jus' got the brilliant idea to have you tell about the funny dream you had last night!

DONNIE: It was also heart-warming.

DUNKLE: It was, indeed - funny and heart-warming!

DONNIE: Should I tell it now?

DUNKLE: Now's as good a time as any!

DONNIE: Well, last night when I went to bed, Uncle Dunkle told me a couple stories and some nursery rhymes . . . and I got very sleepy . . . (BEGINS TO FADE) . . . but I still wanted to hear—

DUNKLE: (FADING UP) . . . and that's the story of "The Old Woman Who Lives in a Shoe" . . . Good night, Donnie.

DONNIE: (HALF-Asleep) Tell me another one, Uncle Dunkle.

DUNKLE: But Donnie, you're almost asleep!

DONNIE: (TRYING TO STAY AWAKE) No, I'm awake. I'm awake.

DUNKLE: Then, how come yo got your eyes closed?

DONNIE: I'm picturing all the wonderful characters in my head.

DUNKLE: Uh-huh.

DONNIE: So tell me another . . .

DUNKLE: Well . . . OK . . . this is the last one, though . . . let's see . . . I got it . . . Humpty-Dumpty sat on the wall, Humpty-Dumpty had a great fall . . . all the king's horses and all the king's men . . . couldn't put Humpty-Dumpty together again. (CHANGE) Donnie? (DOWN) Well, I guess Donnie already 'is' asleep!

SOUND: HIT CYMBAL WITH BRUSH

DONNIE: (FADING ON) Gosh, I should think somebody could put him together.

HUMPTY: (SADLY) All the king's horses and all the king's men tried to put me together . . . and they couldn't!

DONNIE: (AWED) Are . . . are you Humpty-Dumpty?

HUMPTY: You were expecting maybe 'Lil Bo-peep'?

DONNIE: Then, you 'are' Humpty-Dumpty! I heard you had a great fall.

HUMPTY: Yes, little boy . . . and I'm all broken up about it.

"Humpty-Dumpty's Friend"

HORSE: (WHINNY) I'm one of the king's horses . . .

MAN: . . . and I'm one of the king's men . . .

HORSE: . . . and just like Humpty told you, we really wanted to put him together . . . because . . . well . . .

MAN: . . . because we think Humpty is a good egg.

DONNIE: Would you, his friends, mind if I tried to put him together?

HUMPTY: (SADLY) Everybody's tried . . . but it's to no avail!

HORSE: (WHINNY) That means . . . 'It's no use!'

MAN: You don't have to explain it! He knows what 'avail' means!

DONNIE: I . . . I think I can put him back together!

HUMPTY: Everybody's tried . . . it's to no avail!

HORSE: (WHINNY) That means . . .

HUMPTY: It's no use!

MAN: Don't be too sure, Humpty . . . maybe he can do it.

HORSE: I'd like to see you get a break, Humpty!

HUMPTY: A break! Huh-uh! I got broke once . . . and that's enough!!

DONNIE: Look, Mr. Dumpty . . .

HUMPTY: Awe, call me 'Humpty' . . . but it's to no avail!

HORSE: That means . . .

DONNIE: I know . . . 'It's no use!' . . . But look, Humpty . . . I make model cars and I use glue to stick all the different parts together. I'll use some of this glue on you!

MAN: I think, he's 'stuck' on the idea, Humpty.

HUMPTY: (SADLY) Everyone's tried . . . it's to no . . . (UP) . . . Do you really think it would work?!!!

DONNIE: We could give it a try, Humpty!

HORSE: Yeah, what other choice have you got?

DUMPTY: I'll do it! (BEAT) No wait . . . I won't do it. (BEAT) No wait, I'll do it! (BEAT) I won't do it! I can't make up my mind!

HORSE: He's going all to pieces!

DONNIE: That's why I want to help!

MAN: Y'know, Humpty . . . I hear the king's mighty found of omelets!

HORSE: You don't wanna end up the king's breakfast, do you?

MAN: Yeah, remember what 'nearly' happened to "The Three Little Pigs" . . . 'cause they just weren't bringin' home the bacon?

HUMPTY: (BEAT) Well, whatta we waiting for? Bring on the glue!

DONNIE: Here it is! I'll put some on this piece of shell, and stick another piece to it . . . then more glue . . . then another piece. (UP) This is workin' out fine! You're almost finished. (HUMS UNDER)

HUMPTY: Yeah. I'm beginning to feel like my old shell again.

DONNIE: (HUMS) Jus' a few more pieces, Humpty!
(HUMS UNDER)

MAN: He's doin' it! He's doin' it!

HORSE: (WHINNY) He's puttin' him back' together!

HUMPTY: I knew he could . . . all along.

DONNIE: (HUMS, THEN STOPS) There! All done! Humpty-Dumpty is back together again!!

MAN & HORSE: Hooray!!!

HUMPTY: Gee! He did do it! I feel egg-cellent! Grade A! I'm as good as new!!

HORSE: You're better than new!

MAN: He's better than all the king's horses . . .

HORSE: . . . and all the kings men . . .

MAN: . . . put together!

HORSE: Guess the King'll just have to eat oatmeal.

MAN: Well, I guess I'll be gallopin' off . . . on my horsey, I mean!

HORSE: (WHINNY) Yeah. That's me!

MAN: Goodbye!

HORSE: And good luck, Humpty!

SOUND: HORSE-HOOVES GOING OFF

DONNIE: I'd better be goin' too. I'm awfully glad I have met you, Humpty. You're a nursery-rhyme celebrity! I'll drop your name when I get home!

HUMPTY: Just so you don't 'drop' me!

DONNIE:	I'll put you back on the wall before I leave! (EFFORT) There!
HUMPTY:	Thanks, little boy!
DONNIE:	(FADING) Well, g'bye! Maybe we'll meet again sometime . . .
HUMPTY:	Help! Help me! I'm falliiiiiiiiiiing!
DONNIE:	Oh! (EFFORT) I caught ya! Just in time!
HUMPTY:	But . . . to no avail! That means . . .
DONNIE:	I know what it means!
HUMPTY:	Of course you do! But listen, just between you and me . . . I have to keep fallin' off this wall! It is my fate! Each time a child opens up the Nursery Rhyme book to my page - I have to fall off the wall! It is my fate.
DONNIE:	Why?
HUMPTY:	I get too egg-cited!
DONNIE:	Well, I'm gonna fix things so you don't fall down and get broken after I leave!
HUMPTY:	If you can do that, I'll introduce you to 'The Ol' Woman Who Lives in a Shoe' . . . She's a nursery rhyme 'biggie' . . . also!
BONNIE:	Would ya?
HUMPTY:	Indubitably.
DONNIE:	What does that mean?

"Humpty-Dumpty's Friend" 73

HUMPTY: Yes, indeed.

DONNIE: (THINKS) Hey! I know how I can do it! I can use my handkerchief . . . and some string!!

HUMPTY: What's up? You've aroused my curious!

DONNIE: (HUMS, THEN STOPS) There! All finished!

HUMPTY: It looks splendid!! (DOWN) What is it?

DONNIE: It's a parachute, Humpty.

HUMPTY: I knew it all the time.

DONNIE: I'll fasten it on you!

HUMPTY: Oh, joy! And It's my color too . . . 'white'!

DONNIE: There we are! Now, if you fall again, you'll jus' float down to the ground and won't get hurt . . . anymore! You can have as many great falls as you want!

HUMPTY: I'm sittin' pretty now!

SOUND: HIT CYMBAL. WITH BRUSH

DONNIE: And then, I woke up! Well, that's it, Uncle Dunk1e - my funny dream!

DUNKLE: And don't forget 'heart-warming"!

DONNIE: Oh yeah, that too!'

DUNKLE: So? How 'bout I tell ya a story before you go to bed tonight!

DONNIE: (SAD) I guess so.

DUNKLE: What's the matter, Donnie?

DONNIE: Well, I was jus' thinkin' . . . I woke up last night before I had a chance to meet "The Old Woman Who Lives in a Shoe"!

DUNKLE: Cheer up! Maybe you'll meet her tonight!

DONNIE: Yeah! I never thought of that!

DUNKLE: Now, how 'bout a story . . . (PAUSE) Donnie? Donnie, where ya goin'?

DONNIE: (FADING) No time for a story, Uncle Dunkle! I'm going to bed right now! If I'm lucky . . . I can pick up where I left off . . . last night!

"JACK AND THE BEANS TALK"

DUNKLE: Donnie.

DONNIE: Yeah?

DUNKLE: Do you enjoy the stories I tell ya?

DONNIE: Sure, Uncle Dunkle.

DUNKLE: The reason I asked . . . I got to thinkin' the other day . . . about all the stories . . . and how they're mostly about animals – cuz I jus' naturally like animals . . . an' I know you do too . . . and then it came over me, all of a sudden,

	that sometimes I forget . . . or at least, put off tellin' you some of the most famous stories of all time!
DONNIE:	I'm satisfied.
DUNKLE:	I'm glad . . . but today, at this particular story-tellin' session . . . I'm gonna tell you one of the world's most famous stories!
DONNIE:	Uncle Dunkle.
DUNKLE:	Yeah, Donnie?
DONNIE:	I don't wanna hurt your feelings or anything like that . . . but . . .
DUNKLE:	. . . but what?
DONNIE:	But I never heard of it.
DUNKLE:	Never heard of 'what?'
DONNIE:	The famous story you're gonna tell.
DUNKLE:	I haven't told you the name of it yet!
DONNIE:	Oh.
DUNKLE:	It's called 'Jack and the Beanstalk' . . . Well, anyway . . . bright an' early one mornin' . . .
DONNIE:	What about, Uncle Dunkle?
DUNKLE:	What about what?
DONNIE:	What'd they talk about?
DUNKLE:	Who?

"Jack and the Beans Talk"

DONNIE: Jack and the beans.

DUNKLE: Jack and the beans? They didn't talk.

DONNIE: You said they did, Uncle Dunkle.

DUNKLE: What'd you say I said?

DONNIE: You said 'Jack and the Beans <u>talk</u>'!

DUNKLE: (LAFF) No, no, no! I said 'Jack and the Beanstalk!' You see, in this story . . .

DONNIE: What about?

DUNKLE: What about what?

DONNIE: What'd they talk about?

DUNKLE: Who?

DONNIE: Jack and the beans . . . you jus' said they talked! You did, Uncle Dunkle . . . I heard you say it!

DUNKLE: Wait a minute here! Wait, wait, wait! Look, Donnie - that's the name of the story - 'Jack and the Beanstalk!'

DONNIE: You said it again!

DUNKLE: Donnie, would I fib to you?

DONNIE: I guess not.

DUNKLE: Jack did not talk to the beans.

DONNIE: Did the beans talk to Jack?

DUNKLE: No.

DONNIE: Did anybody talk to Jack?

DUNKLE: His mother did. She talked to him.

DONNIE: Good! Now I feel better about Jack!

DUNKLE: Jack and his mother loved each other very much . . . but they were poor . . . and they didn't have any money, either.

DONNIE: That's the worst kind of poor.

DUNKLE: . . .so one day, Jack's mother told him to go sell the cow.

DONNIE: She really gave him a lot of responsibility, didn't she?

DUNKLE: She did, indeed . . . but Jack wasn't much of a businessman. His ability to negotiate a mutually satisfactory deal left much to be desired. He sold the cow to a city slicker for some beans. He said they were 'magic' beans, but when he said it, he out his hand over his mouth, and his shoulders kinda shook . . . and he made a sound that could've been a giggle.

DONNIE: . . .and was it?

DUNKLE: It was! Jack took the beans home to his mother . . . and she became very angry. She threw the beans out the window and sent Jack to bed without his supper!

DONNIE: Did Jack usually take his supper to bed with him?

DUNKLE: He might have on other nights - but not this one . . . he didn't get any supper . . . (UP) What'd you say?

DONNIE: (LAFFS) Gotcha!

DUNKLE: (LAFFS) Guess you did, at that! Well, anyway, Jack looked out the window the next morning . . . and he saw that the beans had grown into a huge beanstalk.

DONNIE:	Ohhh! A beanstalk!
DUNKLE:	That's what I've been tryin' to tell ya!
DONNIE:	Ohhh!
DUNKLE:	Jack and the Beanstalk!
DONNIE:	What'd they talk about?
DUNKLE:	Donnie?
DONNIE:	Yeah?
DUNKLE:	Are you puttin' me on?
DONNIE:	(LAFF) Yeah, Uncle Dunkle! You told me about Jack and the Beanstalk before - you jus' forgot about it. I really had you goin' there for a minute, didn't I?
DUNKLE:	You sure did! (LAFF) Donnie - you are somethin' else!

"JOHNNY THE GIRAFFE"

DUNKLE: Donnie, did I ever tell you about a giraffe named Johnny?

DONNIE: Uncle Dunkle, you never told me about a giraffe - period.

DUNKLE: I never told you a story about a giraffe?

DONNIE: I don't even know what a giraffe is!!

DUNKLE: Oh . . . well (CHUCKLE) . . . a giraffe is a four-footed animal with a long, long neck. A giraffe gets to be three times as high as a man six feet tall - sometimes, a giraffe gets to be as tall as a house.

DONNIE: A giraffe would be a great basketball player!

DUNKLE: Sure would (LAFF)!!

DONNIE: What're you laughin' about, Uncle Dunkle?

DUNKLE: Just thinkin' about somethin' funny (LAFF) - y'know, when your Aunt Rapunzel makes horse-radish cookies with mustard frostin' . . .

DONNIE: Oh, she does not!

DUNKLE: Well, she makes some kind of cookies.

DONNIE: She makes chocolate chip cookies!

DUNKLE: Well, whatever - an' she doesn't want you to get any between meals . . .

DONNIE: . . . or you, either, Uncle Dunkle

DUNKLE: Uh . . . yeah! Well, where does she put 'em?

DONNIE: She puts 'em way up on a high shelf.

DUNKLE: Right! Exactly! (CHUCKLE) That's just what she does! Well, Johnny the giraffe - bein' so tall - could reach the highest shelf his mother had - so d'ya know what Johnny's mother did when she wanted to keep cookies away from Johnny?

DONNIE: What, Uncle Dunkle?

DUNKLE: Well, she'd put the cookies waaaaaay down in the lowest part of the cupboard - with the pots and pans. Because Johnny couldn't bend down that far very easy. (CHANGE) Well, one day, Johnny the giraffe was runnin' along and he heard someone laughin'. He looked around and he saw - Herman, the hyena.

DONNIE: Hyena? Do hyenas laugh, Uncle Dunkle?

DUNKLE: Oh, sure they do . . . sometimes they hire hyenas to make the background laughs for television comedy shows!!

DONNIE: I didn't know that.

DUNKLE: Lotta things you don't know!! Hyenas laugh all the time! Now, the strange thing is - with all their laughin' - the hyenas are afraid of all other animals - and Herman would have been afraid of Johnny - except that . . . (CHUCKLE) . . . except that Johnny looked so funny, runnin' along with his long neck bobbin' back and forth, and his legs flyin' out every which-way!!

HERMAN: (LAFF) Oh, Johnny! (LAFF) You sure look funny. I just can't help laughin' at ya!! I guess it isn't polite to laugh at other folks (LAFF) but I just can't help it!! (BIG LAFF)

DONNIE: Boy! I'll bet Johnny the giraffe didn't like Herman the hyena one bit!!

DUNKLE: Well, now - Johnny wasn't one to hold a grudge. He guessed that maybe he did look kinda funny! And he knew that hyenas laughed at everything - whether it was funny or not! A few days later, Johnny was lopin' along at a fast clip, when he heard someone call his name . . .

HERMAN: (CALLS) Johnny! Hey, Johnny the giraffe!!

DUNKLE: Johnny stopped and looked - and there, tied to the top of a very high tree was Herman the hyena! One end of a rope was tied around him - and the other end was tied to the top of the tree . . . and even though he was in trouble, Herman the hyena couldn't help laughin' . . .

HERMAN: Johnny! (CHUCKLE) I'll tell you how it happened. (LAFFS) I was terrified! (LAFF) It was terrible! Y'see, I saw this

	piece of meat layin' on the ground, y'know? (LAFF) I went over to get it and I stepped into this silly old noose. As soon as I stepped into it, it released the block that was holdin' the top of the tree down to the ground . . .
JOHNNY:	I see, and you got swung way up in the air - and now you can't get down?
HERMAN:	Yeah, that's right - yeah!! (LAFF) . . . and the other animals won't help me 'cause I laughed at 'em (DOWN) just the way I laughed at you, Johnny! (WEAK LAFF) and I'll bet you won't help me either - will ya?
DONNIE:	What did Johnny do, Uncle Dunkle?
DUNKLE:	Well, he kinda looked the situation over and he said:
JOHNNY:	It's just plain natural for a hyena to laugh at folks . . . deep down, you don't mean any harm - and I'm gonna help you!
DUNKLE:	So Johnny stretched his neck way up and untied the knot with his teeth - which released Herman and he fell on the soft ground and wasn't hurt at all!
HERMAN:	Thanks a lot, Johnny! (LAFF) It was sure noble of you to rescue me and I won't ever . . . (STIFLED LAFF) . . . I won't ever laugh at you again!! (BIG STIFLED LAFF)
DUNKLE:	But he had such a hard time tryin' not to laugh that Johnny patted him on the back and said:
JOHNNY:	Go ahead, Herman - go ahead and laugh - laugh your head off. I don't mind. I really don't. You wouldn't be happy if you didn't laugh at the other animals - includin' me.

HERMAN: Thanks. Thanks a lot, Johnny! I really would like to laugh if you don't really mind! (LAFF FADES OFF)

DUNKLE: So Johnny and Herman became sincere, good friends because they understood each other - and accepted each other's ways!!

"LITTLE RED RIDING WHO?"

as told by Uncle Dunkle

DUNKLE: Now, this time, Donnie - I'm gonna tell ya a very famous story. Probably, one of the best-known stories of all time . . . and I wouldn't be at all surprised but that you know it, too!

DONNIE: Does this story start out 'Once upon a time' . . .?

DUNKLE: . . . uh . . . yeah.

DONNIE: Hmm. Sounds familiar - tell me more.

DUNKLE: Well, once upon a time . . .

DONNIE: That's the part that sounds familiar!

DUNKLE: Yeah. Well, anyway - once upon a time there was a little girl . . .

DONNIE: What's her name, Uncle Dunkle?

DUNKLE: I was just gettin' ready to tell ya.

DONNIE: Tell me what?

DUNKLE: What her name was!

DONNIE: What whose name was?

DUNKLE: Red Riding Hood!! She always wore a red hood and a red cape.

DONNIE: Question. Why didn't they call her . . . uh . . .'Red Riding Cape'?

DUNKLE: Well . . . they had a choice - they sort of put it to a vote, y'know - and 'hood' just sorta won out . . .

DONNIE: Oh.

DUNKLE: Anyway, one day Red Riding Hood's mother said: 'Take these goodies to Grandma - she isn't feeling well.'

DONNIE: Red Riding Hood isn't?

DUNKLE: No, no, no, no - her grandma isn't.

DONNIE: Isn't what?

DUNKLE: Feeling well!

DONNIE: Uhhhhhh, (QUICK) Oh yeah!

DUNKLE: So her mother said . . .

DONNIE: The grandma's mother?

DUNKLE: No, Donnie - this was Red Riding Hood's mother!

"Little Red Riding Who?" 87

DONNIE: What'd she say?

DUNKLE: That's what I'm tryin' to tell you!

DONNIE: What?

DUNKLE: What her mother said . . .

DONNIE: What'd she say?

DUNKLE: She said: 'Take these goodies to Grandma and do not talk to the . . .'

DONNIE: Wolf!!

DUNKLE: Wolf. (CLEARS THROAT) Donnie . . .

DONNIE: Yeah?

DUNKLE: Have you - have you heard this story before?

DONNIE: No, it just seemed to be a logical development in the continuity . . .

DUNKLE: I'll – I'll accept that. Anyway, the wolf asked her where she was goin', so . . .

DONNIE: Where who was goin'?

DUNKLE: Red Riding Hood! (BEAT) . . . and she told him . . .

DONNIE: Told him what?

DUNKLE: Where she was goin'!!

DONNIE: Where was she goin'?

DUNKLE: Grandma's house!!

DONNIE: Why?

DUNKLE: To take her some goodies - and she wasn't supposed to talk to him.

DONNIE: To who?

DUNKLE: To the wolf!!

DONNIE: Grandma wasn't supposed to talk to the wolf? Right?

DUNKLE: Donnie, we got a . . . we got a breakdown in communications here! It's a real humdinger! Oh boy! (UP) Red Riding Hood wasn't!! But the wolf said that he was just tryin' to help her.

DONNIE: Help her grandma!

DUNKLE: No . . . uh . . . help Red Riding Hood!!

DONNIE: What was wrong with her?

DUNKLE: Nothing!

DONNIE: Then why was her grandma bringing her goodies?

DUNKLE: She wasn't! Red Riding Hood was bringing goodies to her! And the wolf told Red Riding Hood he was tryin' to help her get there quicker!!!

DONNIE: Get where?

DUNKLE: Grandma's house!!!

DONNIE: (UP) The wolf knew her grandma?

DUNKLE: Well, slightly - yeah!

DONNIE: My grandma doesn't know any wolves!

DUNKLE: Well, believe me - this grandma did!! He told her . . .

DONNIE: Who told her?

DUNKLE: The wolf told her.

DONNIE: Oh. (BEAT) Told who?

DUNKLE: Little Red Riding Hood! He told her about a shortcut . . . but it was really a longer way!!

DONNIE: The wolf lied?

DUNKLE: Yeah, he did! Well, y'see, the wolf wanted to get to Grandma's house first - so he could tie Grandma up, hide her in the closet, put on her clothes, and get the goodies himself!!

DONNIE: Why didn't he jus' - take 'em?

DUNKLE: Huh?

DONNIE: From Red Riding Hood.

DUNKLE: He was a . . . uh . . . he was a dumb wolf!

DONNIE: Oh.

DUNKLE: So Red Riding Hood went the long way and the wolf went the short way - and he did all those things I told you about . . .

DONNIE: What things, Uncle Dunkle?

DUNKLE: About, you know, pretending to be her grandma.

DONNIE: Pretending to be whose grandma?

DUNKLE: Red Riding Hood's grandma!!! She knocked on the door . . .

DONNIE: The grandma did!

DUNKLE: No, Red Riding Hood did!!

DONNIE: Oh.

DUNKLE: And the wolf said: "Come in, dear!' - and she did - and there was the wolf in bed - all dressed up like Ggrandma - and Red Riding Hood said: "Oh, Grandma - what big eyes you have! - and what big ears!! - and what big teeth!!"

DONNIE: Why'd she say that?

DUNKLE: Because . . . uh . . . because she thought the wolf was her grandma!!!

DONNIE: Oh. (BEAT) Let's go watch television.

"LITTLE RED RIDING WHO?"

as told by Aunt Rapunzel

DONNIE: (CALLS) Uncle Dunkle! (BEAT) Uncle Dunkle! Ya home? (BEAT)

RAPUNZEL: (COMES ON) Donnie! My stars! It's Donnie! Of all people! Donnie! My little nephew, Donnie! Donnie, how are you?

DONNIE: I'm fine, Aunt Rapunzel – I had supper with you and Uncle Dunkle last night. I was fine then and I'm fine now. You act like you hadn't seen me for three years.

RAPUNZEL: It does seem like a long time.

DONNIE: It was last night.

RAPUNZEL: When you get older, you lose track of time.

DONNIE: Where's Uncle Dunkle? We had an appointment. He had scheduled a story for me.

RAPUNZEL: He isn't here.

DONNIE: Where is he?

RAPUNZEL: He's out in the backyard – he's building a snowman.

DONNIE: Snowman? But this is July!!

RAPUNZEL: I emphasized that to your Uncle Dunkle, but he was adamant.

DONNIE: Your vocabulary is very anti-Donnie. I don' know what yer talkin' about!

RAPUNZEL: July or not – he's building a snowman.

DONNIE: But there's no snow!!!

RAPUNZEL: No snow – I know. So your Uncle Dunkle went out and bought three hundred snow cones. He'll build it with them.

DONNIE: I'll accept that – (BEAT) Well, I guess I don't get any story today, scheduled or not.

RAPUNZEL: But you <u>do</u>, Donnie – you do, <u>indeed</u>! Aunt Rapunzel will tell you a story – possibly, one of the best-known stories of all time . . .

DONNIE: Does this story start out "Once upon a time..?"

RAPUNZEL: It does.

DONNIE: Sounds familiar.

RAPUNZEL: Well, once upon a time . . .

DONNIE: That's the part that sounds familiar, Aunt Rapunzel.

RAPUNZEL: (UP) Once upon a time there was a little girl . . .

DONNIE: What's her name?

RAPUNZEL: I was getting ready to tell you.

DONNIE: Tell me what?

RAPUNZEL: What her name was!!!

DONNIE: What whose name was?

RAPUNZEL: Little Red Riding Hood! She always wore a little red hood – or a little red cape . . .

"Little Red Riding Who?"   93

DONNIE: Question. Why didn't they call her . . . uh . . . Little Red Riding <u>Cape</u>!!???

RAPUNZEL: Well, they took a vote – they had a choice – and "hood" sorta won out.

DONNIE: Oh.

RAPUNZEL: Anyway . . .

DONNIE: I see . . . the final caucus probably made the difference.

RAPUNZEL: One day, Red Riding Hood's mother said: "Take these goodies to Grandma. She isn't feeling well."

DONNIE: <u>Red Riding Hood</u> isn't?

RAPUNZEL: No, no – her grandma isn't!!

DONNIE: Isn't what?

RAPUNZEL: Feeling well!!

DONNIE: Uhhhhhhh (QUICK) Oh yeah!

RAPUNZEL: . . .so her mother said . . .

DONNIE: The grandma's mother?

RAPUNZEL: No, Donnie – this was Red Riding Hood's mother!

DONNIE: What'd she say?

RAPUNZEL: That's what I'm trying desperately to tell you!

DONNIE: What?

RAPUNZEL: What her mother said.

DONNIE: What'd she say?

RAPUNZEL: She said: Take these goodies to Grandma and . . . do not talk to the . . .

DONNIE: Wolf! Do not talk to the wolf!

RAPUNZEL: Wolf! (BEAT) Donnie . . .

DONNIE: Speaking.

RAPUNZEL: Have you ever heard this story . . . before?

DONNIE: No, the part about the wolf just seemed to be a logical development in the continuity . . .

RAPUNZEL: I'll accept that. (UP – QUICK) At any rate, the wolf asked her where she was going, so . . .

DONNIE: Where who was goin'?

RAPUNZEL: Red Riding Hood! And she told him . . .

DONNIE: Told him what?

RAPUNZEL: Where she was going!!!

DONNIE: Where was she goin'?

RAPUNZEL: To her grandma's house!

DONNIE: Why?

RAPUNZEL: To take her some goodies – and she wasn't supposed to talk to him.

DONNIE: Who's him?

RAPUNZEL: The wolf! The wolf!

DONNIE: Grandma wasn't supposed to talk to the wolf? Right?

RAPUNZEL:	Donnie, what we've got here is a breakdown in communication!! (UP) <u>Red Riding Hood</u> wasn't supposed to talk to the wolf!
DONNIE:	Oh yeah! I get it now.
RAPUNZEL:	Then the wolf said that he was just trying to help her.
DONNIE:	Help her grandma!
RAPUNZEL:	No! Help Red Riding Hood!!
DONNIE:	What was wrong with her?
RAPUNZEL:	<u>Nothing!</u>
DONNIE:	Then why was her grandma bringing her goodies?
RAPUNZEL:	She wasn't!! Red Riding Hood was bringing goodies to her! And the wolf told Red Riding Hood he was trying to help her get there quicker!!
DONNIE:	Get where?
RAPUNZEL:	Grandma's house!
DONNIE:	(UP) The wolf knew her grandma? My grandma doesn't know any wolves!!
RAPUNZEL:	Believe me, this grandma did!!
DONNIE:	Well, there goes the forest!
RAPUNZEL:	He told her . . .
DONNIE:	Who told her?
RAPUNZEL:	Little Red Riding Hood! (LAYS IT OUT) He told her about a shortcut – but it was really a longer way . . .

DONNIE: The wolf . . . lied?

RAPUNZEL: All the evidence seems to point that way! Y'see, the wolf wanted to get to Grandma's house first.

DONNIE: Why?

RAPUNZEL: So he could tie Grandma up, hide her in the closet, put on her clothes and get the goodies himself!!

DONNIE: Why, uh . . . why didn't he jus' . . . take 'em?

RAPUNZEL: Take them?

DONNIE: From Red Riding Hood.

RAPUNZEL: He was obviously a dumb wolf! So Red Riding Hood went the long way and the wolf went the short way – and he did all those things I told you about . . .

DONNIE: What things, Aunt Rapunzel?

RAPUNZEL: About pretending to be her grandma.

DONNIE: Pretending to be whose . . .

RAPUNZEL: (UP) Pretending to be Red Riding Hood's grandma! She knocked on the door!

DONNIE: (UP) The grandma did!

RAPUNZEL: Red Riding Hood did!

DONNIE: Oh.

RAPUNZEL: And the wolf said: "Come in, dear!" . . . and there was the wolf in bed, all dressed up like Grandma – and Red Riding Hood said: "Oh, Grandma, what big eyes you have! And what big ears! And what big teeth!!"

DONNIE: What was the motivation for that?

RAPUNZEL: She thought the wolf was her grandma!

DONNIE: Oh. (BEAT) I'm going out back and help Uncle Dunkle eat the snow-cone-man!!

"MALCOLM THE OLD TIRE"

DUNKLE: Donnie.

DONNIE: Yeah.

DUNKLE: Did you take the trash out in the alley, like I asked ya?

DONNIE: Uh-huh.

DUNKLE: Did you put the lid on the trash-can?

DONNIE: Yep, an' you didn't ask me to either! I took the liberty of doin' it without bein' asked!

DUNKLE: You're a very responsible boy, Donnie - and puttin' the

	lid on the trash-can was good thinkin' on your part . . . 'cause it might rain.
DONNIE:	Paper said it wouldn't.
DUNKLE:	Paper isn't always right. Lotsa picnics have been ruined because people planned 'em from the weather news they saw in the paper.
DONNIE:	Well, anyway, I covered it. (UP) Hey, Uncle Dunkle, sometimes I see funny things out back. I remember when I was a little kid, I saw an old tire on the trash-can down the alley, where the Hendersons live. Then it was gone. I guess the trash man picked it up with the other trash.
DUNKLE:	Donnie, didn't you ever swing on the tire that's hangin' from a rope over at the Hendersons'?
DONNIE:	Sure.
DUNKLE:	Well, gettin' back to trash-cans, I'm gonna tell you a true story.
DONNIE:	What's a trash-can got to do with it?
DUNKLE:	A trash-can is the one who told me the story I'm gonna tell you! The true story, that is - that was told to me, personally, by a trash-can, out back.
DONNIE:	(DISBELIEF) Uh-huh. An old trash-can?
DUNKLE:	Out back!
DONNIE:	An old trash-can out back?
DUNKLE:	I couldn't have said it better myself! (LAFFS) I never did hear of a trash-can that told fibs . . . did you?

DONNIE: I never heard of a trash-can that told anything!

DUNKLE: Well, you're young!

DONNIE: Oh. Uh-huh.

DUNKLE: Anyway, this is the story. A true story . . .

DONNIE: You said that.

DUNKLE: I did?

DONNIE: Several times.

DUNKLE: Well, a couple of months ago - an old automobile tire named Malcolm . . .

DONNIE: Malcolm? That's a funny name for an automobile tire!

DUNKLE: Well, it's as good a name as any. An automobile tire is lucky to have any name at all.

DONNIE: You're probably right.

DUNKLE: Of course I am. Where was I? Oh yeah! This tire named Malcolm woke up and found hisself layin' on top of a trash-can in the alley . . .

DONNIE: Out back?

DUNKLE: Out back.

DONNIE: What was the trash-can's name?

DUNKLE: Trash-cans don't have names (LAFF) That'd be downright silly!!

DONNIE: But if a tire is named Malcolm, why can't . . .

DUNKLE: Well, that's different - when you're a bit older and can do

	a little philosophizin' like your Uncle Dunkle, maybe you'll understand.
DONNIE:	I'll look forward to it.
DUNKLE:	Now, pay attention! Malcolm was surprised as all get-out, 'cause only the day before, he'd been on the left front wheel of Mr. Henderson's car. While he was tryin' to figger it out, Mr. Henderson came and opened the garage door. Then he started up his car and backed it out in the alley. Well, sir - that old tire on the trash-can . . .
DONNIE:	Out back?
DUNKLE:	Out back.
DONNIE:	Malcolm?
DUNKLE:	Malcolm! He called out to his three brothers, Tom, Dick and Montmorency - who were the tires who occupied the other three wheels of Mr. Henderson's car.
MALCOLM:	Hey, you guys! How come I'm on this trash-can, 'stead of bein' on my wheel?
TOM:	I knew we'd have to tell ya sooner or later. It's 'cause Bernice, our sister . . .
DICK:	. . .who used to be the spare tire - and lived in the trunk . . .
MONTY:	. . .has taken your place on the left front wheel!
BERNICE:	That's right, Malcolm! You're all worn out. Your tread is gone. You're an old smoothy! (SNIPPY) Mr. Henderson . . . threw you . . . away!!

MALCOLM: Threw . . . threw me . . . away?!!!

BERNICE: You are a tired out tire! And now I get my chance . . . and I must say, it's about time!! I want to see something of the world. I was getting discouraged, riding around in that gloomy, old trunk!!

MALCOLM: Guess I can't blame you for that, Bernice - but what's to become of . . . me?

BERNICE: I dunno, Malcolm. All I know is . . . that I'm finally going places!!

DUNKLE: Poor old Malcolm! Here he'd served Mr. Henderson faithfully all these years and now he'd been thrown away on a trash-can! The afternoon passed slowly and night came on. Malcolm tossed and turned. He was wide awake. That poor old tire never did retire.

DONNIE: Poor Malcolm!

DUNKLE: But finally morning came - like it always does - the sun rose . . .

DONNIE: Like it always does.

DUNKLE: The little birds began to sing . . .

DONNIE: Like they always does.

DUNKLE: Always _do_!

DONNIE: Oh . . . yeah!

DUNKLE: The rooster crowed - and Malcolm, who had just begun to doze off a little, awakened to find himself right smack

"Malcolm the Old Tire" 103

dab in the middle of some war-whoopin' Indians!! The Indians danced in a circle around Malcolm. There were four of 'em. They weren't very big - and their faces, under the war-paint, weren't red - but white! And several of them, Donnie, had their two front teeth missin'!! Suddenly, the Indians stopped their dancin' and whoopin'. The leader of the Indians motioned to two of his braves, and together they turned Malcolm on end an' rolled him down the alley . . .

DONNIE: Out back?

DUNKLE: Out back . . . Now, even though Malcolm was frightened, he rather enjoyed rollin' along without havin' to support the weight of an automobile. Then the Indians put him down under a big, old apple tree. The leader spoke . . .

BOY: Ugh! 'Big Chief Smog-in-the-Face' wants rope!! Bring rope!

DUNKLE: One of the braves got a piece of rope and the Chief tied one end of it around Malcolm. Malcolm was . . . scared!

DONNIE: Gee, Uncle Dunkle, I'd be scared, too - in a similar situation!!

DUNKLE: Well, Malcolm was good and scared!

MALCOLM: Oh dear! Oh my! Oh goodness gracious! Whatever are they going to do with me?

DUNKLE: One of them climbed the old apple tree - and pulling Malcolm up so he was lifted clear off the ground, he tied the other end of the rope around a big, thick branch. Before

	Malcolm could find out what else they planned to do with him, he heard a woman's voice calling, she said:
WOMAN:	Children! Hurry up! Lunch is ready!!
DUNKLE:	Well!
DONNIE:	(BEAT) Well?
DUNKLE:	Now Malcolm was really confused! After about a half an hour, he looked up and saw, coming toward him, not the 'Indians,' but four, freshly washed little 'boys' - and one of them sounded exactly like the little Indian who asked for the rope!
BOY:	O.K. fellas - now, we'll try out our ole tire swing!!
DUNKLE:	And he put his legs through Malcolm and one of the other boys gave him a push - and he swung way up in the air!!
BOY:	Boy, this is funsville!! This old tire sure makes a keen swing all right!!
DUNKLE:	And then Malcolm realized that he wasn't captured by Indians after all! They were just little boys - playing Indian! One by one, they took turns, swinging on him! - and did Malcolm love it!!
DONNIE:	You're askin' me?
DUNKLE:	No, I'm tellin' ya . . . this was the most fun Malcolm had ever had! It was certainly a lot more fun than riding over hot, dusty roads and gettin' stones in his eyes - and pickin' up nails that took the wind out of him - and goin' round and round so fast that what little scenery he did get to see

was just a blur!! Now, he saw the trees and the birds and the sky - and best of all, the happy faces of the children who loved him!! . . . and, well, that's it, Donnie - that's the true story that the old trash-can in the alley told me . . .

DONNIE: Out back?

DUNKLE: Out back!!

"MURRAY THE MAGPIE"

DUNKLE: Say, Donnie . . .

DONNIE: Yeah?

DUNKLE: Do you remember that time you told me about a dream you had on a desert island - and you saw a giant pink piggy bank?

DONNIE: Uh-huh.

DUNKLE: . . . and then I told about it as a story?

DONNIE: Yeah.

DUNKLE: Well, I had a dream about you . . . and uh . . . I'm gonna tell you about it.

DONNIE: As a story?

DUNKLE: Right! Y'know, it's funny how in real life, one little thing will happen - an' you don't pay much attention to it - and then you dream about it . . . and that one little thing is magnified . . . uh . . . sometimes, it's about somebody you know - and they're doin' bad things that they never really did - but it seems so real when you're dreamin'.

DONNIE: So what did I do bad that made me turn up in your dream?

DUNKLE: I gotta be fair . . . uh . . . what you did was thoughtless . . . uh . . . instead of bein' really bad, y'know?

DONNIE: Uh-huh.

DUNKLE: Remember, the other day when we were goin' to the movies?

DONNIE! Uh-huh.

DUNKLE: . . . and it was time for the picture to start and you were finishin' a candy bar outside?

DONNIE: Uh-huh.

DUNKLE: Well, you were so excited about gettin' in to see the show, that you threw your candy wrapper on the ground! Now, you and I know that you're not a litter-bug . . . and you never have been - and that what you did was a 'no-no' - but these things happen sometimes. We're not perfect, y'know! We can't remember all the time!

DONNIE: Well, how did that get in your dream about me?

DUNKLE: Well, it had to do with not pickin' things up - like the candy wrapper, y'know? It seems that - in my dream - you were stayin' with Aunt Rapunzel and me for . . . oh, say a few months. Your mom and dad were going to Hawaii on a trip . . .

DONNIE: Without me?

DUNKLE: Well, they wanted to take ya, but your mother didn't think you could last the six weeks it would take to get there.

DONNIE: Six weeks! It only takes six hours to fly there!

DUNKLE: Yeah, but . . . in my dream . . . they were gonna swim to Hawaii . . . uh . . . to save money.

DONNIE: But they couldn't swim that far either! Whatta you mean, save money?

DUNKLE: Uh . . .well, so they could afford to check into a cheap hotel when they got there . . . instead of goin' to sleep standin' up in a phone booth.

DONNIE: But why?

DUNKLE: Well, 'cause it would be hard on their feet.

DONNIE: No, no - I don't mean that. I mean, why try to save money? My dad could afford a trip to Hawaii!!

DUNKLE: Uh . . . not in my dream he couldn't, oh no! (CHUCKLE) Do you know how your dad was makin' a livin' in my dream . . . what his job was?

DONNIE: What?

DUNKLE: Sellin' snow cones to Eskimos!!

DONNIE: Huh??

DUNKLE: There's not much money in that, y'know.

DONNIE: How much?

DUNKLE: None.

DONNIE: That isn't very much!

DUNKLE: Well, uh, gettin' back to my dream - you came to live with us but you'd changed. You never picked anything up. At night, you just threw your clothes on the floor - and that's where they'd be the next mornin' . . . and you'd put on fresh clothes. Aunt Rapunzel asked why you didn't pick up your clothes and you said . . . (Now, this is <u>you</u> in the <u>dream</u> - not the <u>real you</u>.)

DONNIE: Oh. I see.

DUNKLE: This is the dream you - and you said:

DONNIE: I will, Aunt Rapunzel - but I'm doin' somethin' else right now.

DUNKLE: But you didn't pick up your clothes - no sir, you did not! And finally, Aunt Rapunzel put her foot down! (BEAT) She'd been holdin' her foot up in the air and I said: 'Why you holdin' your foot up in the air?' - and she got all embarrassed and put it down. And then she told you that she wasn't pickin' up any more of your clothes - they could just lay on the floor forever, as far as she was concerned - and you said:

DONNIE: I will! Later on, I will!

DUNKLE: But you kept throwin' your stuff on the floor, Donnie, and not pickin' anything up - just puttin' fresh clothes on every day, until, pretty soon, your poor Aunt Rapunzel got so upset she just went in the other room and cried . . .

RAPUNZEL: CRIES

DUNKLE: But she didn't cry very long, because - in my dream - she was wearin' cardboard shoes and . . . uh . . . they were gettin' all wet. And I got kinda upset with ya too, Donnie - so I told ya all your clothes were dirty and Aunt Rapunzel wasn't gonna wash 'em and I wouldn't let her wash 'em - so you'd just hafta wear somethin' else - and so you'd have somethin' to wear, I got out some old dresses that your cousin, Wootsy, used to wear when she was your age - and I told you to wear those, until you decided to pick up your clothes!

DONNIE: Dresses! Dresses are for girls!!

DUNKLE: Well, that's all you've got to wear - so put one on! (CHANGE) Well, you did put one on and you were so embarrassed, in case any of the boys would see ya, that you went up to the attic and sulked. Then you noticed a bird's nest on the windowsill. You raised the sash and inspected the nest closely.

DONNIE: Golly, I wonder what kind of bird's nest this is?

MURRAY: Uh . . . it's a magpie's nest.

DONNIE: A bird . . . talked . . . to me!

MURRAY: Murray, the magpie. A hard-workin' bird if ever there was one (SINGS) and there was one - and it's meeeee! (TALK) A point of information - I have imperfect pitch!

"Murray the Magpie"

DONNIE: Uh . . . what're you pickin' up that piece of string for, Murray?

MURRAY: Well, because . . . uh . . . because my business is pickin' up. Here, I'll put it on the nest. Ah, there, that's better. It's hard to speak with a filled-up beak. (UP) Hey, that's a lyric!! (SINGS) It's hard to speak with a filled-up beak!! (TALK) Did I tell ya that I have imperfect pitch?

DONNIE: Yeah. What'd you mean, your business is pickin' up?

MURRAY: Well, magpies, y'see - they make their nests out of all sorts of things, like . . . uh . . . we pick up a string here, a twig there, a leaf, an old, ice-cream-bar-stick, (SINGS) a candy wrapper! (TALK) I . . . uh . . . picked up a candy wrapper yesterday that some kid had dropped at the picture show . . . uh . . . looked somethin' like you. All these things add up - pretty soon, I got a (SINGS) nest!!!

DONNIE: You pick everything up?

MURRAY: Uh, yeah - that's right, little girl.

DONNIE: I'm not a little girl! I'm a little boy! My name's Donnie!

MURRAY: Well, if you're not a little girl . . . uh . . . how comes it you're wearin' a dress?

DONNIE: Well - that's a long story.

MURRAY: I'm sorry I asked.

DONNIE: I'll make it short. Look, I'm wearin' a dress because I wouldn't pick up my clothes and I haven't anything clean to wear.

MURRAY: (SINGS) Oh, shame! Shame on youuuuuuu! (TALK) Oh, that imperfect pitch, it never fails me. Look, all magpies pick things up, and when my little birdies, Denise and Raoul, get bigger - they're gonna learn to pick things up too!

DONNIE: Well, where are Denise and Raoul now?

MURRAY: Uh . . . their mother, Mercedes . . . uh . . . took 'em out to lunch to that new hamburger stand down the street, you've probably seen it - it's there, y'know - it's been there for a couple days now.

DONNIE: Is it a good place?

MURRAY: I just hope it'll be crumby! Listen, Donnie, do what I tell ya, will ya? Pick up your things, because your Aunt Rapunzel and your Uncle Dunkle have a nice nest, too - so pick your things up and . . . uh . . . keep it that way!

DONNIE: Well, thanks for the advice, Murray! Now my business is gonna be pickin' up, too!!

MURRAY: Believe me (SINGS) You won't be sorrrrrrry! (TALK) I still got it - imperfect pitch! (FADES) Well, so-long, Donnie - I'm goin' down to that crumby hamburger stand . . .

DUNKLE: . . . and that's the dream, Donnie - just because you dropped a candy wrapper!

DONNIE: Well, I'm glad. Murray straightened me out. He was really (SINGS) swellllll! (TALK) Hey! I'm not sure but I think I got imperfect pitch!

DUNKLE: (CLEARS THROAT) I'm sure! (LAFF)

"PENNY AND GUINNIE"

DUNKLE: Donnie isn't feelin' so good today, so I'm gonna call him up and tell him a story over the phone . . .

SOUND: DIALING {SEVEN SPINS} - PHONE PICK-UP AT OTHER END

DUNKLE: Surprise! Surprise! Don't say anything, Donnie! This is your ole Uncle Dunkle with a swell story to cheer up the sick boy! I'll just lay the phone on this pillow and speak up so you can hear me good! (CLEARS THROAT) Way down south in the Antarctic regions of the world, where the snow snows and the wind blows, and it's always fifty degrees below zero, lives an amusing little bird called the penguin. The penguin has wings but can't fly, so when he's in the water

... where he spends most of his time ... he uses his wings as flippers and he can zip through the water at twenty-five miles an hour. Think of that! He dives for fish and swims underwater with the greatest of ease. His body is black and his breast is white - and he waddles along like an ice-skater with weak ankles! Once there was a little boy penguin named Penny - and a little girl penguin named Guinnie ...

GUINNIE: Hello, Penny.

PENNY: (SULLEN) Hello, Guinnie. G'bye, Guinnie.

GUINNIE: Where you goin'?

PENNY: I dunno - but if I don't hurry up, I'll be late.

GUINNIE: Are you mad about somethin', Penny?

PENNY: Why should I be mad about somethin'?

GUINNIE: Tell me about it, maybe I can help you - because I'm your friend!

PENNY: Did I give you permission to be my friend?

GUINNIE: (STATEMENT) You don't like me!

PENNY: Sure I like you. (UP) But don't go gettin' any ideas about it! You won't catch me droppin' a pebble at your feet, like some of these other push-over penguins!!

DUNKLE: You see, Donnie, when a boy penguin drops a pebble at the feet of a girl penguin, it means that he wants her to be his girlfriend - but if she doesn't want to be, she just ... kicks the pebble away!

GUINNIE: I'm glad you like me, Penny - but what are you mad about?

PENNY: I'm mad at the Emperor! - thinks he's so smart just 'cause he's three feet tall!!

GUINNIE: The Emperor wouldn't be the Emperor unless he was three feet tall - that's the rule!

PENNY: (SULLEN) Always tellin' us what to do - when to go fishin' - watch out for the polar bears . . .

GUINNIE: That's what the Emperor is supposed to do. He takes care of us.

PENNY: Well, he's not gonna tell me what to do anymore, Guinnie! I've had it! (FADING) G'bye, I'm gonna do a little fishin' over by the iceberg. See ya later!

GUINNIE: It's dangerous around the iceberg, Penny!!!

DUNKLE: But stubborn little Penny headed straight for the iceberg!

PENNY: (FADING ON) Hey, this is more like it! It feels good to be on my own. (CHUCKLE) Nothin' dangerous about an old iceberg! I'll use that big hunk of snow on the iceberg! Bet it's soft. I'm gonna jump on it! Here goes! (EFFORT)

BEAR: GROWL!

PENNY: Oh, oh! I jumped right on top of a polar bear! (NERVOUS CHUCKLE) I got trouble! (UP) Mr. Polar Bear - it's me, Penny the Penguin! Oh, I'm such a dumb sock! I . . . I jumped on top of you because I thought you were a big snow-drift, y'know? You did resemble a big snow-drift (NERVOUS CHUCKLE) and for what it's worth - I apologize!

BEAR: I accept your apology. It was extremely rude of you to

	jump on me. Most animals are scared of me.
PENNY:	I know. I'm one of 'em!
BEAR:	I am pretty mean - mainly because it's expected of me.
PENNY:	Sure, it's your image!
BEAR:	Indubitably! The mothers of the smaller animals get their kids to obey by . . . you know . . . sayin' things like: 'You better stay close to home or the polar bear's gonna get you!!'
PENNY:	That's what Guinnie said to me.
BEAR:	Guinnie's your mother?
PENNY:	Huh-uh - but if she plays her cards right, she might end up bein' my girlfriend.
BEAR:	You know somethin'? There's a lot of polar bears who would consider a chubby little penguin like you a delightful snack for their coffee-break!
PENNY:	Are you gonna have me for a snack?
BEAR:	Uhhhhh . . . no.
PENNY:	(UP - BRIGHTLY) Because you've taken a liking to me, huh?
BEAR:	Partly. (BEAT) I'm also on a diet - very strict!
PENNY:	(SMALL) Oh.
BEAR:	Nothing personal, you understand? You look delicious!
PENNY:	Look, if you like me partly, would you do me a favor? Y'see, I got this possible girlfriend who's crazy about me . . .

BEAR: Oh yeah - Guinnie!

PENNY: See, if I put a pebble at her feet and she kicks it away, I'm gonna look pretty foolish, right?

BEAR: . . . but then, whatta I know about snacks . . . I mean . . . penguins! (LAFF) Whatta ya want me to do?

PENNY: I thought maybe you could make a surprise visit tomorrow and we could have a confrontation – eyeball to eyeball - an' I would step forward and command you to get lost. You'd take off and I'd be a big hero!

BEAR: And your girlfriend, Guinnie, wouldn't kick your pebble?

PENNY: Precisely.

BEAR: And what's in it for me?

PENNY: I jus' won't tell everybody what a big softy you really are.

DUNKLE: So the next day, the polar bear lunged into the penguin camp, growling up a storm!

BEAR: GROWL!

PENNY: Polar bear! Stop that! Stop that annoying growling at once! Can't you see you're scaring my friends!!! Out, out, out!! Or I'll give it to you, good!

BEAR: LIGHT, SHORT GROWL

GUINNIE: Oh, Penny - how brave you are!!

PENNY: All right, all right! That's it, polar bear - on the double now - out, out! Now!!!

BEAR: (SOBS) O.K. O.K. Don't hurt me!! (FADING) I won't ever bother you snacks - I mean, penguins - again!! Don't hurt me!

PENNY: Well, see that you don't! - or it's gonna go hard with ya! (CHUCKLE) I show no mercy!!

GUINNIE: Penny, you were wonderful!

PENNY: Awww! It was something!

GUINNIE: Something? Usually, heroes that I've heard about, say: 'Aw, it wasn't anything.'

PENNY: Yeah, but this was something! The way I handled that polar bear - what verve - what nerve! Incidentally, Guinnie, did you notice that pebble I put at your feet?

GUINNIE: This one?

PENNY: Hey, what'd you kick it for? I did a brave deed! (DOWN) Doncha want to be my . . . my girlfriend?

GUINNIE: You're just another push-over penguin. I might have yesterday, but today I got an offer to appear at the San Diego Zoo. It's really a rare opportunity. (UP) Maybe I'll become a movie star!!

PENNY: I . . . I can't believe it. You actually kicked my personal pebble away. Now I look foolish and I'll never see you again - in that order!

GUINNIE: Aw, Penny - I was just teasing you. The explorer is taking both of us to the San Diego Zoo! (UP) What're you doing?

PENNY: I'm dropping another pebble at your feet.

GUINNIE: And this time, I'm not kicking it away - I'm picking it up!

PENNY: San Diego Zoo - here we come!

DUNKLE: . . . and that's the story, Donnie. How'd you like it? (PAUSE) Donnie? (UP) Huh? You don't sound like Donnie. Who is this? (BEAT) Ajax Laundry? Wrong number? Sorry about that! What? Oh, you say you enjoyed the story? (CHUCKLE) Thanks!

SOUND: HANG UP PHONE

DUNKLE: Now I gotta call up Donnie and tell him this story all over again!!

SOUND: DIALING {SEVEN SPINS} - FADE OUT.

"PEPPY POSSUM"

DUNKLE: In the forests of the south, lives a quiet, friendly little animal . . . with a sharp nose and a long tail . . . called the possum. Not equipped by nature to be a fighter, the possum has another way to protect himself. When trapped by the hunter's dogs, he plays dead - and the dogs leave him alone. Lil Peppy Possum . . . the hero of this story . . . sings about it:

PEPPY: When the dogs are near . . . a possum plays dead
an' he lies flat out like he fell on his head!
He doesn't move a muscle - he's as still as can be!
He's playin' possum jus' t'fool 'im ya see!

>   When the dogs go home . . . possum blinks his eye.
>   Then, he flips his tail, bids the dogs goodbye!
>   But the dogs don't hear 'cause they're far away . . .
>   Ole possum don't care - he likes it that way!
>   That is . . . all possums but <u>me</u>!
>   I'm a lil possum who won't play 'possum' . . .
>   I don't like to stay too long in one place.
>   I'm a lil possum who won't play 'possum' . . .
>   an' I like to lead the dogs a merry chase!!

DUNKLE: Lil Peppy Possum's father worried about his son . . . and, one day, he took him aside for a little talk:

PAPPY: Uh . . . Peppy?

PEPPY: Yes, Pappy?

PAPPY: Peppy, how come you don' play dead when the dogs are chasin' ya?

PEPPY: I jus' don't scare easy, I reckin'. Who's a'scared of an ole hound dog, Pappy?

PAPPY: I can tell ya that, Peppy.

PEPPY: Who, Pappy?

PAPPY: You're pappy, Peppy! Dat's who!

DUNKLE: But Peppy just laughed and ran off into the deepest part of the forest . . . lookin' for danger an' excitement . . . for . . . adventure!

PEPPY: I guess my Pappy means well but he doesn't hafta worry about me! I'm smarter than an ole hound dog!

DUNKLE: But suddenly . . . without warning . . . out from behind a bush . . . jumped Major - one of the biggest, most ferocious hound dogs in the forest!

MAJOR: (BARKS) Well, well, what have we here? Lil Peppy Possum! I do declare!

PEPPY: (NERVOUS) H-h-h-howdy, Major! (BEAT) Well, I enjoyed our little talk but I gotta go now . . . Bye!!

MAJOR: Hold on there, Peppy! (GRABS PEPPY) Urgh! Got ya!! (LAFF)

PEPPY: You leave go of my tail, Major - you hear me! I don't like it!!

MAJOR: An' iffen I don't let go?

PEPPY: Well . . . I reckin' I'll jus' hafta <u>learn</u> t'like it.

MAJOR: I'm a takin' ya home t'my master - he jus' loves <u>possum stew!!</u>

PEPPY: Oh, Pappy! Pappy! Why didn't I listen to you!? You were right an' I was wrong!!

DUNKLE: Peppy . . . not wishin' to become the principle ingredient in a possum stew . . . decided to do something about it . . . He relaxed all his muscles, which made him heavy . . . and hard to drag . . .

MAJOR: (OUT OF BREATH) Here now - how comes it you're so heavy all of a sudden? Don't you go to sleep now - I know your 'possum tricks'!

PEPPY: No, Major - I'm not a sleep . . . but I <u>am</u> sleepy . . . (YAWN) . . . and before long, I'll be <u>sound</u> asleep . . . an' then, I'll be so heavy, you'll never be able to drag me!

MAJOR: Never, huh?

PEPPY: Never - unless you listens t'what I got t'say! I got a plan. (BEAT) Now, about a half mile from here is a lil ole brook . . . fulla nice, cold water.

MAJOR: Nice cold water, huh?

PEPPY: That's right - you go an' get some . . . then, bring it here and throw it on me - that'll make me wide awake . . . and then, you can drag me home.

MAJOR: How do I know you won't run away?

PEPPY: You don't.

MAJOR: Then, I'm not going!

PEPPY: Well, in that case . . . I better get on wit' my . . . (YAWN) . . . sleepin' . . . (SNORES, CONTINUES UNDER)

MAJOR: Wake up, Peppy! You wake up, now, ya here! Iffen ya go t'sleep, you'll be too heavy t'drag home! I'll do what you want! I'll go get the nice, cold water! (RUNS OFF)

DUNKLE: As soon as Major left, Peppy - who wasn't sleepy at all, of course - climbed up to the top of a live oak tree. Here, he waited until Major returned . . .

MAJOR: (COMING ON) Hey! Hey, you! Peppy Possum! You comes right outta that tree! I've got ya some nice, cold water!

PEPPY: (OFF) I'm sorry I caused you all this trouble, Major . . . but I don' need it anymore! (LAFF)

MAJOR: Ohhhh, Peppy!! You make _me_ tired!!

PEPPY: Tired, eh? (BEAT) Then, throw the water on yourself! I feel fine!!!

>This lil possum was sure scared t'day
>an' I thank my stars that I got away!
>Dogs chase a possum - it's their nature too . . .
>So a possum's gotta do what he's gotta do!
>Oh, I've learned that dogs are somethin' t'fear!
>When they're around, I better stay clear . . .
>Or else I'll play dead as my pappy advised . . .
>Playin' possum's not bad, I jus' realized!!!

"PERKY THE PIG"

DUNKLE: Perky. Uh-huh, Perky.

DONNIE: Hmm?

DUNKLE: Perky.

DONNIE: What's Perky, Uncle Dunkle? I hope you don't think I'm unreasonably inquisitive.

DUNKLE: Not at all. Perky was his name. Well, one day . . .

DONNIE: Whose name?

DUNKLE: Why, the little pig I'm gonna tell you about. Yes sir, this . . . is the tale of a pig.

DONNIE: Perky is a funny name for a pig!

DUNKLE: Well, Perky was a funny little pig - with a funny little tail. Full of life, he was, and a day wouldn't pass but what his mother'd have to scold him for fightin' with the other pigs or for playin' past his bedtime. He didn't mean to be naughty. He just had a lot of energy (which is kinda unusual - for a pig. Generally, they just like to lie around and sleep!) . . . but like I say, not Perky. He wanted to be up and doin' all the time. He wanted to be 'with it' - you know what I mean?

DONNIE: I know what you mean.

DUNKLE: . . .and he thought his mother was mean when she scolded him. So one day, he was walking along by himself and he thought:

PERKY: Other pigs' mothers don't scold them as much as mine does, I betcha, I betcha, I betcha! No sir! Sometimes, I have the distressing feeling that she doesn't like me at all, I betcha. I betcha, I betcha!

DUNKLE: . . .and suddenly, Perky stood stock still - and stopped grumbling - didn't say a thing for a whole minute. He jus' looked and looked . . .

DONNIE: What was he lookin' at, Uncle Dunkle?

DUNKLE: Himself.

DONNIE: Himself?

DUNKLE: Himself! He was lookin' at a reflection of himself in a quiet, placid mud puddle he liked to roll in. He wasn't lookin' at all of himself, either. He was starin' at his tail! At last, at last, he thought, he'd discovered why his mother didn't like him!

PERKY: So that's it! So that's why! Um-hmm, I bet it is! My mother picks on me 'cause my tall is straight - and not curly, wurly, wurly like the other pigs, I betcha, I betcha, I betcha! (BEAT) Hmm! Maybe I'm . . . uh . . . maybe I'm not a pig!

DUNKLE: That puzzled him plenty for a while, and then he made a decision.

PERKY: If I'm not a pig, what am I? I'll do a little investigating and find out what kind of an animal I really am. Uh-huh, that's what I'll do - I'll do that - Um-hmm!!!

DUNKLE: Well, Perky hadn't eaten his breakfast, so he was able to squeeze under the double gate of the pigsty fence and off he went to find out what he truly was. First off, he went 'round the corner to the chicken-yard, and called to old Mrs. Hen, who was scratching for something to eat.

PERKY: Mrs. Hen, let me in the chicken yard . . .

HEN: (CLUCK) Who is it?

PERKY: It's me, Perky, the pig, uh, I mean, Perky. Just Perky. Perky, the 'nothin'', the way things stand now. I'm not at all sure I am a pig, 'cause my tall is straight and all the other pigs have curly tails. Your tail is straight and I thought maybe (UP) I'm a chicken!!

HEN: (CLUCK) Don't be silly, Perky - my tail's got feathers on it, so you can't be a chicken. Have you got fine feathers like mine?

PERKY: Well . . . no.

HEN: (CLUCK) Well?

PERKY: I guess I'm not a chicken!

DUNKLE: Then Perky thought he might be a horse - so he skedaddled over to the barn to see Harold the horse . . .

PERKY: Harold! Hey! Look at me! It's Perky, down here by your feet, right here! Look, uh, I'm of the opinion that I'm a horse, instead of a pig, understand?

HAROLD: Uh . . . no.

PERKY: My tail, see? It's straight like yours, Harold. It's not as long. It'll probably get longer as I get bigger . . .

HAROLD: Not only that - you'll grow too - and when you get to be a biggggg horse (if you are a horse) you'll be able to pull the heavy farm wagon.

PERKY: The heavy . . . farm wagon! (WEAK LAFF) Excuse me, Harold - I have suddenly decided that I'm not a horse after all . . .

DUNKLE: Perky didn't like the idea of pulling any heavy old farm wagon, so he went over to see the sheep who lived on the great pasture. He saw the lambs playing, so he started to play right along with them . . . and he spoke to one of them . . .

PERKY: Hi! My name's Perky and I used to be a pig. But I'm not anymore, 'cause my tail is straight and all the other pigs have curly tails and you know . . . you know the bit!

SHEEP: Mmmmaybe you're a sheep like mmmme. It's true, you don't have wool like mmmmme - but then mmmmaybe you've been sheared already.

PERKY: Sheared!!! What (and I'd just as soon you didn't tell me) is that?!!

SHEEP: When you have a lot of wool on your back, the mmmmmen come with big shears and cut all the wool off - and spin it into thread - then you grow mmmmmmore wool and they cut it off and spin it, and then you grow mmmmore . . .

PERKY: Wait! Wait! Wait a minute!! Let's get this straight! Look! If I was a sheep (GULP) - they'd cut off . . . I mean, they'd shear me? But I haven't any wool - and if they tried to cut off my hair, they wouldn't get much. I . . . I don't think I'd like to be a sheep, so . . .

SHEEP: Look! Here comes the shearing mmmmman now. Would you like to audition your wool for the mmmmmman?

PERKY: What 'wool'? - 'bye!!!

DUNKLE: That little Perky wasn't takin' any chances on being sheared, so he high-straight-tailed it back to the pigsty, which was the safest place he knew. As he was squeezin' under the gate, his straight tail got caught in a crack and stuck. Perky grunted, and struggled to get loose - and then suddenly . . .

SOUND: BOING

DUNKLE: His tail was loose - and whatta ya know! He'd pulled so hard, he stretched his tail clear out and it snapped back right . . . into . . . a real, authentic curly pig's tall. So now his misgivings were all over. He felt like a pig - he thought like a pig - and now, he for the first time - looked like a pig!!

PERKY: Let's face it! C'mon (HEE-HEE) I am a pig!!

"PETE THE PELICAN"

DUNKLE: This is the story of Pete, the Pelican, Donnie. Now a pelican looks somethin' like a swan . . .

DONNIE: Somethin' like a swan?

DUNKLE: Yeah, except his neck is a great deal shorter and his beak is about five times as long - and his beak has a pouch where he holds the fish he catches . . .

DONNIE: Uncle Dunkle, I think any self-respecting swan would get very uptight over that description of a pelican!

DUNKLE: So, let him get a good lawyer and sue me! When a pelican's flyin' over the ocean and sees a fish swimmin' along in the water below, he swoops down and scoops the fish up in his beak.

DONNIE: That's dinner-time, eh, Uncle Dunkle?

DUNKLE: Nope! Huh-uh - no sir! Instead of swallowing it right then and there, he lets it land 'plop' in this pouch I was tellin' you about, under his beak. And before the day's over, ole Pete's got ten, maybe twelve fish in his pouch to take home to his family - and ole Pete used to sing this song . . . if you can call this singin' - it's pelican singin'!

PETE: To a pelican, fishes are really delicious.
We'd rather eat fishes than steak!
A pelican's eyes are trained to see - what he sees - in the sea . . .
Fish are the things he loves to see - in the sea - you see!
So, so to keep in condition, we'll all go out fishin' . . .
It really can't be beat!
I might say, in addition, the fishes are wishin'
We'd turn our attention to meat!!

DUNKLE: Pete the pelican enjoyed fishin' very much and everything would have been just fine, if it hadn't been for that old pest, Hobo the Hawk!!

HOBO: I'm Hobo the hawk! Hobo, that's me! I like fish too - but I'm just too darn lazy to catch any myself. So what do I do? I'll tell ya! I work it like this! At night, when ole Pete the pelican's flyin' home with his pouch full of nice, fat fish - I play a dirty trick on him (LAFF). Here's what I do - I fly way up above him, and then, without any warning at all, I zoom down at him!! - just like a dive-bomber!! Scares ole Pete somethin' awful! (EVIL LAFF) Ole Pete opens his mouth real wide to yell - and then, quick as a wink, I grabs me a fish from his pouch - and fly away - fast!!

DUNKLE: Hobo the hawk made life miserable for Pete the pelican, and the worst part of it was that ole Pete couldn't figger out any way to get even with Hobo. (CHANGE) Pete visited Lester the lobster, his friend, and Lester said:

LESTER: I can live in the water - I can live on land. I'm lucky that way. (SIGH) But I sure wish I could fly like you, Pete! I'd like that! That, I'd like!!

PETE: But Lester - you know lobsters can't fly!!

LESTER: I know that - that I know! It's impossible, but I'd like to try it anyway. I'd like that. That I'd like - I'd like that!!

PETE: Wait a minute!

LESTER: What's on your mind, Pete? Huh, what? What, Pete, what, huh? What? Huh? Pete, what?

PETE: I just figgered somethin' out - a way for you to fly - and at the same time help me teach Hobo the hawk a lesson! You do what I tell you now. You crawl into my pouch - and then I'll tell you what to do when Hobo the hawk tries to steal a fish!!

DUNKLE: So Lester did what Pete told him. He crawled into Pete's pouch. Then Pete spread his big wings and flew high up in the sky. It wasn't long before ole Hobo the hawk appeared, smackin' his beak in anticipation . . . all set to steal another fish from Pete the pelican. First, he climbed up high - then he dive-bombed at Pete! Pete opened his beak

	just like before, but when Hobo poked his beak into Pete's pouch (LAFF), there was a big surprise waitin' for him!!!
PETE:	(SHOUTS) Now, Lester, now!!!
DUNKLE:	Lester the lobster threw his big green claws around Hobo's neck and held on tight!
HOBO:	Hey! Cut it out!! What's goin' on here!! Watch it!!!
DUNKLE:	Hobo tried to fly away, but the weight of Lester around his neck made him top-heavy - and he zig-zagged all over the sky! Well, Hobo looked so scared and confused that Lester the lobster felt sorry for him. So, after he figgered Hobo had learned his lesson, Lester released his hold and fell down, down, down into the ocean below!!! Hobo was a scared hawk all right - and he wasted no time flyin' home! (PAUSE) Later, when Hobo got to thinkin' of how silly he musta looked, bobbin' up and down in the sky with a lobster hangin' onto his neck, he burst right out laughin'!
HOBO:	(LAFF)
DUNKLE:	And the next day, when he saw Pete the pelican sunnin' himself on a big rock, Hobo flew down to him and said:
HOBO:	Hi, Pete! Hi! I just wanted to tell you that I was a pretty scared ole Hawk yesterday!! You taught me a good lesson, you did! I felt awful stupid flyin' around with a "lobster necklace" on!!!
PETE:	You did look pretty silly, Hobo! (LAFF)
HOBO:	Yeah! After this, I'll catch my own fish! I won't ever steal from you. (UP) Pete?

PETE: Yeah, Hobo?

HOBO: I . . . I never had any friends . . . and . . . I wanna be your . . . friend!

PETE: It'd be a pleasure!

DUNKLE: So Pete the pelican forgave Hobo the hawk and they became very, very, very, very good friends - and everyday, if you happen to be near the ocean, you can see them up in the sky - fishin' together!!!

"PUNKY POSSUM'S MUD BATH"

DUNKLE: Say, Donnie . . .

DONNIE: Yeah.

DUNKLE: Did I hear your Aunt Rapunzel scoldin' you about somethin'?

DONNIE: Uh-huh, I was out playin' in the mud . . .

DUNKLE: Well, why doesn't she watch ya, instead of standin' on her head on the flagpole!

DONNIE: Oh, she was not!

DUNKLE: Well, she was doin' somethin'!!

DONNIE: Well, anyway, I got mud all over my new pants.

"Punky Possum's Mud Bath" 137

DUNKLE: That's not so good - even with all the new ways of gettin' clothes clean nowadays.

DONNIE: I just didn't think about it. I was playin' and it was muddy - and then I was muddy, an . . .

DUNKLE: Say, did I ever tell you about Punky Possum and the mud bath?

DONNIE: Never did! Not that one. Tell me about Punky Possum, Uncle Dunkle!

DUNKLE: Well, way down south lives Punky Possum. Unlike most possums, Punky's pappy for instance (who likes to sleep a lot), Punky loves to frolic around the forest and have a high old time for himself. Sometimes, he even goes off on an adventure at the nearby farm - which is full of mud-puddles - and his idea of fun is . . . well, listen!

PUNKY: This lil possum likes the mud might-i-ly
An' you donno the fun a puddle full o' mud-'ll be!
Water's for the ducks . . . but not for me!
This lil possum like to be mud-dy!
Play in the mud from morn til night,
You should see me, I'm a sight!
And so you'll know it's me all right - Scrape the mud
 away!!!
Oh, boy! Look at all the little ole mud puddles!!! This
 is most enjoyable! It's like takin' a bath wrong end to
 - 'stead of gittin' clean - I gits dirty!!!

DUNKLE: Punky's mother was very concerned by her son's love of mud-puddles. She kept a tidy house, like most mothers, and Punky disrupted everything!! She said:

MAMMY: My Punky earned my trust when jest a lil guy,
An' when he gits so dirty, there's a reason why.
Like all the other boys - mud is what he most enjoys.
He's muddy as a big mud pie!!
I never really worried where my Punky'd play,
'til he came in all covered with that mud, one day!
In trackin' up the floors - he doubled all my chores!
Punky shouldn't do me that way!!

PUNKY: (COMING ON) Mammy! Hey, mammy! I'm home!

MAMMY: Well, if I didn't recognize your voice, I do declare I'd a-never knowed who 'twas! You git that mud offen you now, hear?

PUNKY: I haven't got much mud on me!

MAMMY: Punky, you're about the muddiest lil ole possum around hear! Everybody's talkin' 'bout ya!!

PUNKY: Well, ya gotta admit, mammy - I am makin' a name for m'self!!

DUNKLE: Punky didn't mean to do wrong, but he loved the mud so much, and played in it so often, that finally even his sleepy ole pappy noticed it.

PAPPY: You in trouble, boy!
Lil Punky and his clothes
're caked with mud but I suppose
To him there's more where he got those!
(DOWN) But duds aren't buds the oak-tree grows!
Lil Punky, don't you see,
Has never paid a laundry fee,

	He jest assumes they clean for free!

	He jest assumes they clean for free!
	To prove they're downright neighborly!!
(CALLS):	Hey, Punky! You hear me, Son? You're in big trouble, boy! You come on along over here where I'm sleep . . . uh . . . where I'm a-restin'!
PUNKY:	(COMING ON) Howdy, lil ole pappy! I hear you callin' me?
PAPPY:	I shore rightly was - 'cause you in trouble, boy! You come along home 'cause we got a lil . . . uh . . . talkin' to do . . . out back . . . in the woodshed!
PUNKY:	Man possum to man possum?
PAPPY:	Uh-uh. Man possum to <u>boy</u> possum!
PUNKY:	That's what I was a-feared of! (BEAT) Oh, well - on the way back to the house, we can carry us in some wood!
DUNKLE:	So Punky and his pappy went home to the woodshed and in the olden days a woodshed usually meant . . . a spankin'!! Pappy opened the door - and they went inside!
PUNKY:	Well . . . uh . . .
PAPPY:	Well!
PUNKY:	Well (BEAT) Hear we are inside the lil ole woodshed, lil ole pappy!
PAPPY:	Don' you go givin' me any more of' that <u>lil ole pappy</u> stuff, lil ole Punky!!
PUNKY:	(STALLING) Reason I called you 'lil ole pappy' - lil ole pappy, is 'cause you is kinda 'lil' - ole pappy!!

PAPPY: Desist!! 'I' is not the subject of this confrontation - you is.

PUNKY: Lemme jist git one thing straight - you gonna confront me - or spank me?

PAPPY: I is gonna confront ya!

PUNKY: Oh, that's good news! You jus' didn't have the heart to spank me, did ya?

PAPPY: I got the heart - but my hand has got small bones! Now, you listen at me, Punky - you're in trouble, boy! This mud-puddle playin' has gotta stop!!

PUNKY: But I love mud-puddles! Can't I jist sorta . . . taper off?

PAPPY: Huh-uh.

PUNKY: Jist wondered.

PAPPY: I'm a-gonna be fair with ya, Punky - you go on back over by the mud-puddles, and if you can find a good reason for a possum gittin' all muddied up like you does, I won't say nothin' more about it . . . (UP) Oh, an' Punky!!

PUNKY: Yes, lil ole pappy?

PAPPY: Talk with a pig about mud! See what he says.

DUNKLE: So Punky went back over to the farm. There were the lovely mud-puddles, and right in the middle of the biggest one . . . was . . . a pig!

PUNKY: Howdy, Mr. Pig!

PIG: GRUNT!

PUNKY: What're you talkin' - French?

PIG:	Of course not! That's just a sound I make when I'm enjoyin' the mud.
PUNKY:	I never make that sound.
PIG:	Why should ya - you're not a pig.
PUNKY:	But I like the mud!
PIG:	Possums don't need mud - jist gits 'em dirty.
PUNKY:	Git you dirty too!
PIG:	But I'm a certified pig and mud is my friend. I got me a couple good reasons for likin'' it!

> Air-conditioned I am not,
> When the sun is high and hot,
> So the mud's my favorite spot,
> Keeps me cool all day!
> Tho I lack insecticide,
> When the flies torment my hide,
> Mud again is on my side - keeps the flies away!!

... and those are two good reasons for a pig likin' mud!! Pigs don't just like to be dirty. Mud is a heap of protection from the hot sun and insects.

PUNKY:	I never thought of it that way. Well, so-long, Mr. Pig! You taught me a good lesson! It comes down to this: mud is for pigs but not for possums!
PIG:	Well said!!
DUNKLE:	And then Punky went back home. He found his pappy and mammy waitin' for him. Dinner was hot on the table - but before he sat down, Punky said:

PUNKY: This lil possum gave up mud - it is true,
'cause now I know the good a puddle full o' mud'll do!
Mud is for the pigs - but not me too,
My mud-puddlin' days are really through!
Swing in the trees from morn til night,
I'm so clean – it's outta sight!
I'm glad I finally saw the light - No more mud - no way!!!!

"RAPUNZEL AND THE BANDIT"

DONNIE: Hey, Uncle Dunkle, I jus' got a great idea!

DUNKLE: What's that, Donnie?

DONNIE: How 'bout ya tell me about how you met Aunt Rapunzel!!

DUNKLE: Well, O.K. (BEAT) Uh, didn't I ever tell ya that one?

DONNIE: Sure you did . . . long time ago . . . I'd jus' like t'hear it again!

DUNKLE: You wanna hear it again.

DONNIE: Yup.

DUNKLE: How I met Aunt Rapunzel?

DONNIE: Yup.

DUNKLE: Again?

DONNIE: Yup.

DUNKLE: You wanna hear it?

DONNIE: Yup.

DUNKLE: You don' wanna hear about Punky Possum or Perky Pig?

DONNIE: Yup. I mean, nope!

DUNKLE: How I met Aunt Rapunzel?

DONNIE: Uncle Dunkle?! You're stallin'!

DUNKLE: (LAFF) O.K. I'll tell ya the story of how I first met dear Aunt Rapunzel.

DONNIE: Good.

DUNKLE; But before I do, I just have one question, Donnie.

DONNIE: Shoot!

DUNKLE; How's it go?

DONNIE: Don't you know?

DUNKLE: Well, it was a long time ago.

DONNIE: I'll get ya started.

DUNKLE: That sounds fair.

DONNIE: One time . . . when you were a young dude . . . you went to . . .

DUNKLE: A 'dude' ranch!

DONNIE: No, Uncle Dunkle! Think! Think!

DUNKLE: Sure seems like it was a dude ranch.

DONNIE: It's a place where they make 'cheese'!

DUNKLE: Cheese? Let's see, cheese is made with 'milk' . . . and milk comes from 'cows' . . . and cows live on . . . <u>a dude ranch!!</u>

DONNIE: I give up! Go ahead, Uncle Dunkle! Tell me about the dude ranch!

DUNKLE: Thought ya'd never asked! (CHANGE) See, I was stayin' at this dude ranch one time . . .

DONNIE: I had a feelin' it began that way.

DUNKLE: . . . and the ranch hand's daughter was kidnapped by a 'bandit'! The ranch hand's daughter's name was . . .

DONNIE: Rapunzel.

DUNKLE: How'd you know?

DONNIE: Lucky guess.

DUNKLE: And the bandit's name was . . . (PAUSE)

DONNIE: Was what?

DUNKLE: I thought you were gonna try and guess.

DONNIE: I'll pass this time.

DUNKLE: The bandit's name was Wyatt Twerp. Know why?

DONNIE: 'cause he was jus' a little guy?

DUNKLE: Right! And he hated anythin' big and beautiful!

DONNIE: Why?

DUNKLE: 'cause he was little and funny lookin'!

DONNIE: Why'd he steal Aunt Rapunzel'?

DUNKLE: 'cause she was big and beautiful! . . . and 'cause her father owned the biggest cows and horses . . . and the biggest ranch in those parts!

DONNIE: What 'parts' were they?

DUNKLE: Simple. The parts that I was in at the time!

DONNIE: Naturally. (BEAT) So why didn't Wyatt Twerp steal the horses and cows too?

DUNKLE: He figgered it was easier to steal a helpless female . . .

DONNIE: You better not let Aunt Rapunzel hear you call her 'helpless'!

DUNKLE: Oops! Oh yeah . . . Don't tell her I said that! She might lift me over her head . . . and put me on the branch of a tree out back . . . and make me sleep on it . . . again!

DONNIE: She never did that!!

DUNKLE: But she might! (CHANGE) Anyway, Wyatt Twerp figgered if he kidnapped Rapunzel . . . he could ransom her off for the cows and horses . . . and the ranch itself!

DONNIE: Gosh! He was a real 'mean' dude!

DUNKLE:	That's why he wanted a <u>dude</u> ranch! To be mean on! And he wanted the horses and cows to be mean to!
DONNIE:	What about Aunt Rapunzel?
DUNKLE:	If he'd been mean t'her, she'd've lifted him over her head . . . and put him on the branch of a tree . . . and made him sleep there!
DONNIE:	Then, why didn't she?
DUNKLE:	'cause the mean ole bandit had tied her up! So the ranch hand . . .
DONNIE:	What was <u>his</u> name?
DUNKLE:	Rapunzel's Father.
DONNIE:	Makes sense.
DUNKLE:	So he hired me to rescue Rapunzel . . .
DONNIE:	Why didn't he go and rescue her?
DUNKLE:	'cause he had no way of gettin' to the top of the high, rocky mountain cliff where Rapunzel was bein' held captive!
DONNIE:	So you climbed the mountain?
DUNKLE:	No . . .
DONNIE:	Why not?
DUNKLE:	Well, I had no way of gettin' up there either! That mountain was unclimbable!
DONNIE:	Then, why did he hire you?
DUNKLE:	Y'know, I never did figger that part out!

DONNIE: How did Wyatt Twerp get up there?

DUNKLE: If I'd have known that . . . I'd've gone up the same way!

DONNIE: How did ya get up there?

DUNKLE: Well, I didn't . . . for a long time . . . I might never have . . . if it wasn't for this eagle I met . . .

REGAL: D'Artanyan!

DUNKLE: Who said that?

REGAL: It's me . . . Regal the eagle!

DUNKLE: Where are you?

REGAL: I'm flying up above! (BEAT) Wait, I'll come down.

SOUND: WINGS FLAPPING

Ah! There we are. You remember me, D'Artanyan.

DUNKLE: Why, sure I do! You're the eagle that Wyatt Twerp was shootin' at last week!

REGAL: That's right. And you saved my life.

DUNKLE: Well, all I did was distract him while you got away.

REGAL: It was very brave of you!

DUNKLE: (LAFF) It was, wasn't it!

REGAL: He might've shot you, instead.

DUNKLE: Naw! He only hates things that are big and beautiful, like you!

REGAL: I flew down to visit you because I saw you standing out

	here - and you look upset. What's wrong?
DUNKLE:	The ranch hand's daughter was kidnapped by . . . guess who!
REGAL:	Wyatt Twerp, that mean little twerp!
DUNKLE:	That's where he got his name.
REGAL:	Why don't you go get him!
DUNKLE:	That's why I'm upset! The ranch hand hired me to save his daughter, Rapunzel . . .
REGAL:	Nice name.
DUNKLE:	. . .only Twerp has her tied up atop that great big . . . unclimbable mountain over there!
REGAL:	You mean Mount Unclimbable?
DUNKLE:	That's the one! I just don't know how I'm gonna get to the top of it!
REGAL:	This one's too . . . too easy! I'll fly you up there!!
DUNKLE:	Would ya?
REGAL:	Sure. I owe you a favor!
DUNKLE:	. . .and so, Donnie, Regal the eagle gently grabbed a hold of my dude ranch 'duds' . . . and together we flew up to the top of Mount Unclimbable. During the flight, we thought up a foolproof plan. Regal dropped me off 'round the back of the shack where the fair Rapunzel was bein' held. Then, he flew 'round the front of the shack. Regal flew 'round and 'round in circles . . . makin' a whole mess

of noise!

SOUND: BIRD CAWS, WINGS FLAPPING

DUNKLE: Finally, when mean ole Twerp came out with his pistol to shoot the big, beautiful eagle, I went into the shack through the back door, untied Rapunzel . . . and we waited out in the back. Regal - who was fightin' mad - flew 'round distracting Twerp. Finally, when the bandit had run out of bullets . . . an' was plumb tired to boot . . . Regal the Eagle swooped down, grabbed Twerp up, and took him off to jail! Rapunzel and I waited on the mountain for Regal to come back. It was at the time that we fell in love! Regal came back, took us both down to safety . . . and soon Rapunzel and I were married!! And guess who was our best man?

DONNIE: A mouse.

DUNKLE: Right! No! No, it wasn't a mouse at all! It was Regal the eagle!!

DONNIE: Uncle Dunkle?

DUNKLE: Yes, Donnie?

DONNIE: Last time you told me that same story . . . it wasn't a dude ranch . . . it was a cheese shop! . . . and it wasn't a bandit named Wyatt Twerp . . . it was a gang of cheese-stealin' mice! . . . and it wasn't an eagle who saved the day . . . it was a security guard mouse!

DUNKLE: Yeah, but if you take away the part about the bandit . . . and the eagle . . . and the dude ranch . . . whatta ya got?

DONNIE: The story of how you met Aunt Rapunzel.

DUNKLE: Exactly what you asked for! (LAFF)

DONNIE: (GIGGLE) Oh, Uncle Dunkle, you're somethin' else!

DUNKLE: I know.

"REDDY ROBIN AND THE OWL"

DUNKLE: My nephew, Donnie, and I are great pals - and one of my special pleasures is tellin' him a bedtime story every night. And usually, Donnie falls off to sleep before I'm half-finished - but last night (FADE) he gave me a peck of trouble - a peck and a half (FADE IN) . . . and the poor, but brave woodcutter married the king's daughter and they lived happily ever after. G'night, Donnie!

DONNIE: That was a swell story, Uncle Dunkle! Tell me another one!

DUNKLE: Another one! But Donnie, that's the third story I told you and they were long ones, too!

DONNIE: Aw, come on - tell me another one - then another and another!

DUNKLE: Why, Donnie - that'd take all night!

DONNIE: I know it. I'm gonna stay up all night like a grown-up does! I'm not sleepy and I'm not goin' to sleep!

DUNKLE: Well, suit yourself, Donnie - but I think the sandman'll have something to say 'bout this 'fore the night's over, you old night-owl, you! (BEAT - UP) Say! Did I ever tell you about the little baby robin that tried to stay up all night - that wanted to be a night-owl?

DONNIE: No, Uncle Dunkle - you never! Tell me that one!!

DUNKLE: O.K. This is the last one, though. This one's about little Reddy robin. Reddy robin was just a little baby - and one day, when his folks were out lookin' for food, he decided he was old enough to try a bit of flyin' - so he perched on the edge of the nest and . . .

REDDY: This is it! Today I fly! One for the money - two for the show - three to make ready and four - to GO!!!

DUNKLE: Little Reddy robin dipped and whirled about - losing his balance - finding it again - and after a while getting pretty tuckered out, just lookin' for a place to light! Suddenly, he spied a strange nest - and made for it just as fast as he could fly!

REDDY: (EFFORT) Just a little farther - a little more (EFFORT)

	There! I made it! It's not our nest - but it is a nest and I guess it'll be O.K. if I just rest up a bit. (BEAT) Hmmmm! Not bad. Not bad at all. Well, me for a little shut-eye! (YAWN) I'm sleepy!!!
DUNKLE:	So little Reddy robin had a snooze - and when he woke up he was still alone. He was hungry - and he missed his parents. He wanted to fly back to their nest but he was so weak from hunger that he didn't dare try. Several days passed. And little Reddy was getting weaker and weaker. What was worse, bein' just a baby like I told ya, he soon forgot about his parents - forgot who they were. Now he was really alone! Suddenly, he looked up and saw a huge bird, with big, round eyes, approaching the nest!!
REDDY:	Oh, what a big bird! And it's comin' to this nest, I know! I'm scared!!
DUNKLE:	The big bird, with the large round eyes, came closer and closer - and landed kerplunk! - right on the edge of the nest!
OWL:	Ahhh! It's good to be home again!
REDDY:	(MEEKLY) Hello.
OWL:	Hoo!
REDDY:	Me!
OWL:	Hoo!
REDDY:	I said, it's me!! I kinda forgot what my name is.
OWL:	Young fella, when I say 'Hoo' - I don't mean 'Who?' I

	mean 'Hoo!' It's a thing owls say. You could verify this by checking it in the owl manual.
REDDY:	(UP) Oh, then if you're an owl - this must be an owl's nest!
OWL:	That's good sound logic . . . yeah.
REDDY:	And if I'm in an owl's nest, I must be an owl!!
OWL:	I don' wanna hurt your little feelings, but you do not look like any owl I have ever seen.
REDDY:	Aren't you my papa?
OWL:	Hoo!
REDDY:	You!
OWL:	Hoo-boy! Sorry, kid - but huh-uh!!
REDDY:	Well, I'm pretty sure I am an owl, so what I'll do! I'll adopt you . . . as my papa!
OWL:	I don' think you are an owl, but you look pretty skinny to me, so I'll take care of you.
REDDY:	. . . and you'll be my adopted papa?
OWL:	Yeah! I'll be your adopted papa!!!
DUNKLE:	So the papa owl took care of little Reddy robin, who by now thought he was a sure-enough 'hooty-owl.' The first night things kinda went like this.
OWL:	Look, I'm goin' out to hunt field mice now - so you'd better get some sleep, lil bird.
REDDY:	Hoo!

OWL: You - that's who!!

REDDY: When I say 'Hoo' - I don't mean 'Who?'- I mean 'Hoo!' It's a thing owls say!!

OWL: You're a growin' bird - you gotta get your sleep!

REDDY: I'm a growin' baby owl! Owl's don't sleep at night, so I'm not goin' to! So there!!

OWL: You wanna know something, kid? You just think you're an owl!

REDDY: I'm an owl. I'm stayin' up!

OWL: O.K. Listen to this approach. Owls sleep in the daytime. Did you sleep today?

REDDY: No.

OWL: Why not?

REDDY: I . . . uh . . .wasn't sleepy.

OWL: Suit yourself. I gotta go get those field mice. G'bye!!

REDDY: Silliest thing I ever heard of!! A lil old baby owl, not bein' . . . (YAWN WORD) a-a-able . . . to stay awake all night! I'll show . . . my papa . . . my (YAWN) papa . . . (BEAT - SNORE)

DUNKLE: And little Reddy robin fell fast asleep. (YAWN) Gosh, I'm gettin' sleepy myself, Donnie - excuse me!! Well, papa owl, 'stead of lookin' for field mice, decided to look for Reddy's mama and papa. He checked with all the birds in the forest and finally he heard about some robins who'd lost their little boy. (YAWN) He went to see the robins and sure enough, they were Reddy's parents!! The owl took them back to his nest and the robins carried the sleeping Reddy back to their nest. (YAWN THIS LINE) So when Reddy woke up, he found himself back with his real parents - and he remembered who they were - and who he was and was very contented and happy!!

REDDY: Oh boy!!! Now that I'm not an owl, I can sleep at night. This stayin' up all night isn't for the birds - except owls!!

DUNKLE: (VERY SLEEPY) It isn't for Uncle Dunkles either!! (YAWN) . . . and that's the story of the little robin who thought he was . . . an . . . owl. How'd you like it, Donnie? . . . Donnie? Well, whatta ya know! Donnie's not as big a night-owl as he . . . thought . . . he was. He's fast (YAWN) asleep . . . and I think I am . . . too . . .

"SHERLOCK SNAIL FINDS A HOME"

DUNKLE: Say, Donnie, did you ever talk with a snail?

DONNIE: Gosh! No, Uncle Dunkle, never did . . .

DUNKLE: The octopus hadn't either.

DONNIE: What octopus was that?

DUNKLE: The one in the story I'm about to tell you.

DONNIE: Oh, that octopus.

DUNKLE: See, the octopus lived in the Atlantic Ocean . . . right off the coast of the British Isles. And he was a very curious little octopus, indeed - so he was always travelin' around and

"Sherlock Snail Finds a Home" 159

lookin' at everything around him! Now, the snail, on the other hand, lived in the Mediterranean Sea . . . and he was even a more curious type. He always wanted to see what a real ocean looked like . . . So it was only natural that eventually these two very different looking creatures would meet. When they did . . . this is what happened . . .

OCTOPUS: I say, old chap, I'm an octopus . . . I'm quite sure of that . . . but I'm not certain as to exactly what you are.

SHERLOCK: My name is Sherlock . . . and I know you're an octopus . . . because you have eight arms . . . I read books, you see . . . something that you obviously do not or you'd know what I am!

OCTOPUS: I'll see if I can guess! Hmm, you have a shell on your back . . . so therefore . . . you must be a . . . turtle!!

SHERLOCK: (INSULTED) I am <u>not</u> a turtle!

OCTOPUS: Then, what might you be?

SHERLOCK: I <u>might</u> be a bald eagle - but, in point of fact, I'm not. I, dear friend, am what is commonly referred to as a 'snail' . . . Sherlock snail, to be exact. And this "shell" on my back, as you call it, is my home! I curl up in there . . . to sleep.

OCTOPUS: I sleep in a cave.

SHERLOCK: I know. I read the books that fell off passing ships and float down – so I've seen pictures. You look smaller in person.

OCTOPUS: I'm about average. Most of us octopi are this size. We're only BIG in the movies!

SHERLOCK: Hmm. That I didn't know.

OCTOPUS: I thought you read.

SHERLOCK: I must've skipped that page. (CHANGE) Well, this meeting certainly was a noteworthy experience.

OCTOPUS: Quite so. But I must be getting back to my cave before dark.

SHERLOCK: Ah, that's where I have the advantage! I can just curl up in my shell-style house on my back! Quite convenient! No fuss!

OCTOPUS: Yes, quite so, quite so.

SHERLOCK: So I shall be here - on this very spot - tomorrow morning.

OCTOPUS: I'll come back and visit you . . . if you like.

SHERLOCK: I like it quite well. I shall see you then.

DUNKLE: But the next morning, when the octopus returned . . . to his surprise . . . Sherlock snail was nowhere in sight! On the very spot where he had met his new friend the night before was now a little worm!

OCTOPUS: I say, worm - have you seen what is commonly referred to as a 'snail' around here?

SHERLOCK: I am not a worm! I wasn't a turtle yesterday and I'm not a worm today! I told you, Mr. Octopus, I am a snail!

OCTOPUS: You're the very same "snail" I met yesterday?

SHERLOCK: I am indeed.

OCTOPUS: But . . . but what has happened to your shell-type home?

"Sherlock Snail Finds a Home"

SHERLOCK: Why, it's on my back . . . of course.

OCTOPUS: Oh no, it isn't! I'm afraid you've lost your home!

SHERLOCK: (UP) Y-y-you're right! My shell is gone! Oh, dear! Oh, dear! What is a snail without his shell!?

OCTOPUS: A worm?

SHERLOCK: I don't like being a 'worm!' But worse than that - where shall I sleep tonight when it gets dark?

OCTOPUS: You may make my cave your home!

SHERLOCK: That's extremely kind of you - but I couldn't. I hardly know you. I'd feel as though I were imposing.

OCTOPUS: Not in the least. After all, we are in the same family!

SHERLOCK: Oh no, we're not! I am a snail - even without my shell - and you are an octopus, remember?

OCTOPUS: I've got you there, Sherlock! We are both in the mollusk family! Both snails and octopi are mollusks. (UP) We're cousins! (DOWN) I've been doing a bit of 'reading' my-self!

SHERLOCK: But I don't have eight arms - like you!?

OCTOPUS: They are called tentacles. I read that too!

SHERLOCK: Really? Well, since we are related - I guess it would be all right to share your cave.

DUNKLE: So the snail and the octopus moved in together . . . and became the very best of friends!

DONNIE: But did Sherlock ever find his shell, Uncle Dunkle?

DUNKLE: Oh, sure! He found it! The very next day! The water current had swooped it off his back . . . and it was hiding behind a large piece of coral. Sure he found it, Donnie! But y'know what?

DONNIE: What?

DUNKLE: Even after he found his shell - the snail and the octopus decided to continue to live together in the cave . . . because they enjoyed each other's company! (LAFF) And that's the story of how 'Sherlock Snail Found a Home!' (BEAT) How'd ya like it, Donnie?

DONNIE: Gee, it was swell, Uncle Dunkle!

DUNKLE: Good! (BEAT) Now, tomorrow, Donnie, I'll tell ya the story of how 'Sherlock <u>Holmes</u> Found a <u>Snail</u>!!'

"STICKY WICKET"

DONNIE: (FADING ON) Hi, Uncle Dunkle! I'm here! (BEAT) Uncle Dunkle? Anybody home?

DUNKLE: (FADING ON) Donnie! Oh, Don! Oh, there you are! Sorry that I'm late!

DONNIE: Where were you, Uncle Dunkle? Did you forget your story-tellin' appointment?

DUNKLE: I left the door open for ya.

DONNIE: I found that out.

DUNKLE: Sure you did! Your Aunt Rapunzel is in the other room makin' pickled ice cream.

DONNIE: Oh, she is not!

DUNKLE: Well, she's doin' somethin' . . . Donnie, I was out for the purpose of purchasin' some tickets for you and me.

	We're goin' to the circus tomorrow afternoon (LAFF)!!
DONNIE:	We are?!!
DUNKLE:	Say, I haven't told you a new circus story lately, have I?
DONNIE:	Huh-uh.
DUNKLE:	Well, we'll take care of that (CHUCKLE) right now! This circus story took place in merry old England, and it really concerns a family of trained seals - you know, the animals who balance all sorts of things on their noses.
DONNIE:	They make funny noises, too.
DUNKLE:	Yeah! Sort of a bark. Well, this particular family of seals would have been the greatest act in show business . . . except for one thing . . .
PAPA:	(BARK) Coot Ya know, missus, you and I are, without a blinkin' doubt, two of the most outstandin' trained seals in the United Kingdom - if not the entire world. I'm not braggin', neither. It's just the simple truth, as I knows it! I mean, why be guilty of false modesty - we're the best!! . . . but I do wonder sometimes about our son, Wicket.
MAMA:	(QUIET) Here! He's standin' right beside us! No cause to hurt 'is feelin's, love!!
PAPA:	'e knows what I mean. (UP) Wicket!
WICKET:	(BARK) Yes, Dad?
PAPA:	Wicket, yer heart's not really in show business, is it, lad?
WICKET:	Oh, it is, sir! It is, indeed! But me nose - it's got no talent! I can't balance no matter how hard I tries!!

DUNKLE:	The trainer would teach the seals to catch all sorts of things on their noses - and papa and mama seal could catch and balance anything and everything - but not so Wicket! To make it easier, or so he thought, the trainer threw a large ball to Wicket. It bounced off the end of his nose and Wicket exclaimed . . .
WICKET:	Here, watch it! What's idea of smackin' a bloke on the tip of his nose with a blinkin' ball like that!?? I got me a sensitive nose, I have!! It's black, so you won't see the nasty bruise - but it'll be there, make no mistake about that!
DUNKLE:	The trainer had an Irish temper and he was exasperated with Wicket. He shook his finger at him and said:
TRAINER:	Here, you, Wicket!! Either you learns to balance somethin' . . . anythin' . . . on yer nose . . . or it's off to the zoo with you! Ye can cavort in the pool and lie about in the sun all the live-long day . . . barkin' yer head off at the tourists . . . and nobody will know that you've got a no-talent nose! So shape up, Wicket! Shape up! . . . or I'm gonna have to ship you out!!
DUNKLE:	That was an ultimatum!
DONNIE:	An ulti-whattum?
DUNKLE:	An ultimatum. It meant that either Wicket learned to balance things on his nose like the other seals - like his mom and dad, or he'd end up in the zoo!!
DONNIE:	What so bad about the zoo? The zoo's O.K.
DUNKLE:	That's what Wicket said to his dad.

WICKET: (BARK) I say, Dad - what's so blinkin' bad about the zoo? I'll get me three square meals a day (UP) Well, actually, they're more in the shape of a fish - but I won't have any worries - and you won't have to worry about me!

PAPA: And ye'll be outta show business for good!! The glamour, the applause, the gay, wonderful feelin' of bein' a celebrity - of bein' loved by one and all!! Our family has been in show business for three generations - ever since Admiral Percy Barrington Posh, the explorer, brought your great-great-granddad home from the North Pole!! And he was a hero, he was! One time, Admiral Percy Barrington Posh was lookin' for the North Star through his sextant and it slipped through his blinkin' fingers and would have rolled offen the deck right into the ragin' sea, if it hadn't a been fer your great-great-granddaddy catchin' it . . .on the very tip of nose!! . . . and because of that, he was knighted by the Queen herself!! Sir Wicket Seal!!

WICKET: Sir . . . Sir . . . Sir Wicket!!

PAPA: That's right! His name was Wicket, too. You was named after him - and now, yer disgracin' us all - your great-great-granddaddy an' yer old mum and dad with your no-talent nose!!

WICKET: (BARK) I say, help me, Dad! Toss some things at my nose - let me try again - teach me, Dad!!

PAPA: Here, catch this cabbage!

WICKET: Owwww! Me poor little nose! (UP) Oh, it's no use, dad, it bounces right off! I've had it! It's off to the zoo for me!

DUNKLE: He'd given up - poor Wicket!

PAPA:	Well, we're gonna miss you, Wicket - your mum and I - because, well, because we loves ya . . .
MAMA:	Travelin' about in the circus won't be the same without you, dear!
PAPA:	Oh, we'll write letters to each other and all like that, but . . .
MAMA:	. . .but it's not the same - not the same, love, as bein' together . . .
DUNKLE:	Wicket had given up on goin' with the circus, when the trainer, who wasn't a bad sort, thought that Wicket should be given just one more last chance. He had brought his little girl to the circus with him and she was carrying a bag of marshmallows. The trainer had a bag of golf balls - and he was going to toss a golf ball to each of the seals, papa, mama and Wicket. If Wicket balanced one on his nose, he could go with the circus. That was the deal. (BEAT) Well, he tossed a ball to papa seal . . .
PAPA:	BARK
DUNKLE:	. . .then to mama seal . . .
MAMA:	BARK
DUNKLE:	. . .and then he reached around to take another ball from the bag, but his (LAFF) silly little girl held out her bag of marshmallows - and instead of a ball, the trainer took out a sticky marshmallow . . .
SOUND:	DRUM ROLL
DUNKLE:	He tossed this to Wicket and it stuck to his nose!

SOUND: CYMBAL CRASH

WICKET: The golf ball! I caught the golf ball right on the end of me no-talent nose!! I finally did it!!

DUNKLE: Well, Wicket thought for sure that his nose had come through at last!! He did flip-flops and rolled over and over and over and still the object on his nose stayed put! It didn't fall off! The trainer was amazed! Also papa and mama seal!

TRAINER: I'm amazed!

PAPA: I'm amazed, likewise!

MAMA: Oh, I'm amazed too, love!

DUNKLE: But the trainer's little daughter was laughin' fit to kill. She told her father that it wasn't a golf ball, that it was her marshmallow that had stuck to Wicket's nose!!

TRAINER: Marshmallow, was it? Well, our little Wicket may be a no-talent balancer, but he's a great little comedian! I never seen nothin' so funny in my life! (LAFF) We'll star Wicket in the show with that sticky marshmallow bit! - and he'll be a comedy sensation!!

WICKET: I finally did it!

TRAINER: We'll bill him as 'Sticky Wicket'!!!

SOUND: CYMBAL CRASH

DUNKLE: ...and that is how Wicket the seal not only got to stay in show business, but became a comedian and a great star!!

DONNIE: (BEAT) Did he get to eat the marshmallow?

"THE BIG WIND"

SOUND: WIND - FOLLOWED BY DOOR SLAM

DONNIE: The wind is really blowin' up a storm today, Uncle Dunkle! It's snuggy to be indoors where it's nice and warm!

DUNKLE: You think this is a wind? (LAFF) I guess you never heard about the 'big' wind.

DONNIE: The . . . the 'big' wind?

DUNKLE: Well, it happened a long time ago - a little fella (kinda like you) was out flyin' his kite - 'cause the wind was high and the air was clear. His kite was way up in the clouds and it was most truly a kite-flyer's kind of day. Barnstormer . . .

DONNIE: That was the little boy's name!

DUNKLE: No, no - that was the kite's name.

DONNIE: He called his kite . . . 'Barnstormer?'

DUNKLE: Barnstormer Pfaff - that was the kite's name. Now, I'm sure you'll agree that Cadwallader or Demetrius would have been downright silly names!!

DONNIE: Pretty silly names for a kites, uh-huh - but Uncle Dunkle, I jus' never heard of a kit havin' a name!

DUNKLE: Well, you have now. The little boy's name was Eddie. The wind lifted his kite . . .

DONNIE: Barnstormer!

DUNKLE: Barnstormer Pfaff! . . . higher and higher until finally it lifted Eddie clear up off the ground and soon he was way over the trees - sailin' free as a bird. This was exciting and Eddie was enjoyin' it until he realized that eventually he'd have to come down and (CHUCKLE) where would that be?

DONNIE: . . . and where would that be, Uncle Dunkle?

DUNKLE: As it turned out, it was on top of a mountain - waaaaaaay up there! So after puttin' Eddie down, the kite . . . Barnstormer . . .

DONNIE: Pfaff . . . Barnstormer Pfaff . . .

DUNKLE: Oh yeah! (CHUCKLE) Well, he soared away for further adventures . . . and Eddie began to wander about - but he'd never been this high on a mountain before and soon he realized that he was lost - good and lost. He wandered every which way - aimlessly - just to keep on doin' somethin' - so he wouldn't be scared, y'know?

DONNIE: I'd be scared!

DUNKLE: So would I!! Well, before long (but you'd be more scared than I would . . . be . . . y'see!) Well, before long, he came to a pine forest. He entered it slowly and looked all around. He was frightened - and night was comin' on . . .

DONNIE: I'd hate to have been in his shoes!

DUNKLE: Well, he was barefoot, actually. Suddenly, he heard a voice . . . a gruff voice . . .

BEAR: GROWL!

DUNKLE: It cautioned him not to be afraid - that he was a friend. The boy looked behind him and there was a big . . . bear!

BEAR: Cool it! Hey, you look all uptight. I won't hurt ya! Bears in stories never hurt ya – but in real life, in Yellowstone Park, for instance . . . Oh, I wouldn't trust one of us bears for two consecutive seconds!!

EDDIE: You mean, this is a . . . dream?

BEAR: No, this isn't a dream. This is 'real life' - but it's story 'real life' - not 'real life real life' - you know what I mean?

EDDIE: That's kinda confusin'!!

BEAR: You come with me for the night. I'll take care of you . . . and then in the mornin', I'll walk you home. Besides, I want you to meet my wife and son. (CHUCKLE) They're real folks!!

DUNKLE: So Eddie went along with the big bear and they went to the big bear's house. Once inside, by a warming fire, he met Mrs. Bear and Sonny, the little bear.

SONNY: C'mon, Eddie - I'll show you around. See, here's our towels. They're marked 'His', 'Hers,' and 'Who Else?' (UP) Hey, do you like honey?

EDDIE: Honey? Sure!!

SONNY: My pop and I love honey! Mom uses Saccharine. She's trying to knock off about three hundred pounds - wants to trim to a neat six hundred and fifty pounds. (BEAT) Hey, you wanna know somethin'? I'm getting' sleepy. Let's you and me turn in, huh? C'mon, you can wear a pair of my sleepers!

DUNKLE: So Eddie and Sonny went to sleep. The next mornin', Eddie was up bright and early, anxious to get started toward his home in the valley. Mama bear insisted that he should have a good breakfast first, so she fixed some porridge. But Eddie, impatient to get started, said the porridge would be too hot and he didn't want to wait. So the bears decided to take him home at once so he could have breakfast with his folks. Papa bear said:

BEAR: By the time we get back, the porridge will be cool enough to eat . . .

DUNKLE: So they started off. As they neared the foothills, close to the valley floor, a little girl passed them.

GIRL: Hi, little bear!

EDDIE: Hello, little Goldilocks!!

DUNKLE: The little girl continued up the path. Sonny bear was quite excited as he'd never seen a little girl this close before - but Papa bear said:

BEAR: Take a real good look, Sonny. You'll never see her again!

DUNKLE: . . .and the bears and Eddie continued down the path as the girl, Goldilocks, went up the path toward the home of . . . the three bears!

"THE CHERRY TREE CAPER"

DONNIE: Hi, Uncle Dunkle!

DUNKLE: Hi, Donnie! Come on in! Good to see ya! Hey, I got a special story for ya today. It's about history.

DONNIE: (UP) History! Oh boy, Terrific! I like history! (DOWN) . . . but not very much.

DUNKLE: You sounded pretty enthusiastic there for a minute.

DONNIE: Well, bein' enthusiastic doesn't cost me anything . . . or take up much of my time . . . or cause me any inconve-

	nience . . . so I figger if it'll make a favorite 'Uncle' of mine happy . . . what the hey!
DUNKLE:	What the hey, indeed! I appreciate such soul-searchin' compassion. You're a good boy!
DONNIE:	(SOTTO) I know.
DUNKLE:	Hmm?
DONNIE:	Nothin'.
DUNKLE:	Now let's get back to that historical story . . .
DONNIE:	'Historical story' - Hey, that's nicely put!
DUNKLE:	Well, you know I pride myself on my 'put nicelies.'
DONNIE:	I'm aware of that.
DUNKLE:	Today's story is about a strong, stalwart, dedicated man of destiny - name of Washington . . .
DONNIE:	Washington <u>who</u>?
DUNKLE:	George Washington . . .
DONNIE:	So who was he?
DUNKLE:	He was the father of our country . . . and the very first President of the United States. Well, when he was just a little guy like you, George's father . . . this being his birthday and all . . .
DONNIE:	His father's birthday?
DUNKLE:	George's birthday - and his father gave him something he was sure George was gonna like . . .

DONNIE: What was it?

DUNKLE: I was just gettin' ready to tell ya.

DONNIE: Tell me what?

DUNKLE: What his father was gonna give him.

DONNIE: What was his father gonna give him?

DUNKLE: A little hatchet, and he told him . . .

DONNIE: George told him?

DUNKLE: No, no, no . . . now, listen . . . George's father told George to be careful and not to cut himself with the hatchet. Well, he flailed that hatchet about . . . cuttin' everything in sight . . . and finally . . . do you know what he cut?

DONNIE: Something that wasn't out of sight?

DUNKLE: He cut down his father's favorite cherry tree! . . . and when his father came home . . . what was the first thing he saw?

DONNIE: His home?

DUNKLE: Well, sure - but besides that!

DONNIE: The hatchet.

DUNKLE: (UP) Right! He saw the hatchet . . . (TAKE) No, he didn't! He saw the cherry tree . . . lyin' on the ground . . .

DONNIE: Did a hue and cry go up?

DUNKLE: . . . and with great sorrow, he said, 'Who has cut down my favorite cherry tree?'

DONNIE: Did a hue and cry go up?

DUNKLE: A hue and cry, Donnie, like you wouldn't believe! And everybody said they didn't know anything about it.

DONNIE: ...anything about what?

DUNKLE: The cherry tree that George'd cut down.

DONNIE: George who?

DUNKLE: George Washington.

DONNIE: Oh yeah.

DUNKLE: ...and he said, 'I cannot tell a lie...!!'

DONNIE: His father couldn't?

DUNKLE: No, no, Donnie...no...George said that. His father frowned. 'It was I who cut down your favorite cherry tree...I did it with my little hatchet...'

DONNIE: His father did?

DUNKLE: No! George said that!

DONNIE: ...said he cut his father.

DUNKLE: No, said he cut down the cherry tree!

DONNIE: George's cherry tree?

DUNKLE: ...uh...no. (CLEARS THROAT) Donnie...

DONNIE: Yeah?

DUNKLE: Why doncha go out in the kitchen with Aunt Rapunzel?

DONNIE: Why?

DUNKLE: I thought maybe you two could whip up some mustard fudge or something.

DONNIE: Hey, that sounds yummy! (CALLS) Aunt Rapunzel - here comes trouble!!

"THE ENCHANTED TAPE RECORDER"

DUNKLE:	Donnie, when I mention an evil magician . . . whatta you see?
DONNIE:	Uh . . . sort of a . . . thin guy?
DUNKLE:	Could be. What else?
DONNIE:	Tall, maybe?
DUNKLE:	Good.
DONNIE:	Wearin' a shiny black suit . . . an' ya know what the shiniest parts are . . . the knees and the elbows.

DUNKLE: <u>Very</u> good.

DONNIE: A cape . . . sort of over his shoulders. (UP) Red lining! (ENTHUSED) Carryin' a brass-headed cane . . . shaped like a cobra's head!

DUNKLE: I guess you just about covered it.

DONNIE: . . .but there's another thing about evil magicians, Uncle Dunkle. He'd have to have a skinny little black mustache . . . kinda turned up on the ends and like out to a point . . . gotta have that!

DUNKLE: . . .and that's the way you'd picture an evil magician.

DONNIE: Um!

DUNKLE: Well, there's lot's of stories with magicians in 'em who looked just like what you described . . . you're very observant for your age.

DONNIE: I was observant before I even had any age on me! Even in the crib, I didn't miss anything!

DUNKLE: What you gotta be aware of, though, is that appearances can be deceiving. What you described could be the way a regular, nice person looked, too. Eccentric, maybe . . .but nice. You see, the evil is really in the mind . . .where there's no clothes or mustaches or canes to make a person suspicious and on the look-out for danger. Now what is all this leading up to?

DONNIE: Yeah, what <u>is</u> this leading up to?

DUNKLE: The story I'm gonna tell you today . . . it's called 'The

Enchanted Tape Recorder' . . . and it was owned by a magician.

DONNIE: (IMPRESSED) An enchanted tape recorder!

DUNKLE: But this magician didn't look anything like the one you described.

DONNIE: You mean, I did that for nothin'?

DUNKLE: No. Here's a quarter!

DONNIE: (CHUCKLES)

DUNKLE: What I mean is . . . I was getting you in the mood for the story and the fact that it's gonna be about a different type of evil magician.

DONNIE: Verbosity's a lot easier when you're retired, isn't it?

DUNKLE: There is more time for it, right! Well, this magician's name was Kazam. Al A. Kazam. He was short and roly-poly.

DONNIE: Mustache?

DUNKLE: No mustache. He wore large, horn-rimmed glasses and sort of walked around on tippy-toes all the time . . .

DONNIE: Why?

DUNKLE: Maybe his heels hurt.

(THEY BOTH CHUCKLE.)

. . .an' he'd look from side to side, as if expectin' somebody to jump at 'im . . . and he giggled all the

	time . . . even if nothin' funny was being said or happenin'. He took himself very seriously . . . and he expected people to go out of their way to give him exactly what he wanted.
DONNIE:	. . .and what if they didn't?
DUNKLE:	Then he'd play one of his tricks on 'em! He was about four hundred years old.
DONNIE:	Gee.
DUNKLE:	He took very good care of himself . . . got medical check-ups every year . . . and he didn't look more than three hundred and fifty . . . and a young three hundred and fifty at that!
DONNIE:	I wanna hear about his enchanted tape recorder!
DUNKLE:	Sure ya do! I was goin' on and on there - maybe I shoulda just said he was fat and selfish and let it go at that. Anyway, one day he was tip-toeing down the street and he looked down and saw a nickel. He picked it up and headed for Mr. Arbuthnot's store, his intention being to purchase a bar of candy.
SOUND:	DOOR OPENED - BELL TINKLE - DOOR CLOSED
ARBUTHNOT:	I am Arnold Arbuthnot. May I help you?
KAZAM:	Do you always introduce yourself to a customer? First name and all? (GIGGLE)
ARBUTHNOT:	To new customers, I do. I've never seen you before. It just seemed a common courtesy.

KAZAM: My name is Kazam.

ARBUTHNOT: Kazam.

KAZAM: Al A. Kazam! I'm a musician . . . uh . . . I mean . . . magician. (GIGGLE) I always get those two mixed up! I travel all over . . . buzzing around to different places - lighting hither and yon. (GIGGLE)

ARBUTHNOT: I am a mercantile person. I operate an establishment for the retail sale of commodities . . . the buying of which fills my coffers with the monies of the multitudes.

KAZAM: If I take your meaning, you mean . . .?

ARBUTHNOT: I mean, did you want to buy something?

KAZAM: No beating around the bush there!

ARBUTHNOT: I am very busy! Did you want to buy something?

KAZAM: I'm the only one in the store.

ARBUTHNOT: Establishment!

KAZAM: Whatever.

ARBUTHNOT: I'm ready to close up . . . I'm expecting out of town guests at home . . . and you've tried my patience!!

KAZAM: Try mine, sometime!! You'll like it! (CHANGE) You have won me over with your charm! (GIGGLE) I'll take one of those candy bars in the case there - that one!

ARBUTHNOT: That'll be ten cents . . . and hurry it up . . . I'm closing!

KAZAM: Ten cents?

ARBUTHNOT: Ten cents! Do you want the bar or not?

KAZAM: I only have a nickel! (IDEA) Look! I'll only eat five cents worth of the bar!

ARBUTHNOT: Good day, sir!

KAZAM: (GIGGLE) Lemme have the candy bar! I want people to go out of their way to give me what I want!!

ARBUTHNOT: I'll stay right here and I won't give you what you want. No candy bar!! Out! Out!

DUNKLE: So the musician . . . I mean, magician . . . put his tape recorder down on the candy-counter. He waved his wand over it, magically and . . .

KAZAM: Ta-ta! I'm leaving this tape recorder! I hope you have lots of luck . . . all bad! (GIGGLE)

DUNKLE: Mr. Arbuthnot didn't notice at first. In fact, he'd decided to pay no more attention to Al A. Kazam . . . and was going about his business. When he was ready to close the shop, he looked on the counter and saw the tape recorder. He remembered the little fat man and the connection became apparent. He knew who the tape recorder belonged to.

DONNIE: Good for him.

DUNKLE: Then Mr. Arbuthnot noticed a brass plate on the side of the tape recorder. It read: 'Property of Arnold Arbuthnot. The last recording on this tape recorder will come true.' This didn't make too much of an impression on him . . . but his greedy little soul realized that he had come by a tape recorder without any expense to himself . . . and he remembered that his son, Darwell, had always wanted a tape recorder . . . so he put it in his car and took it home with him.

SOUND: DOOR OPEN - CLOSE

ARBUTHNOT: Martha! Darwell! I'm home! Daddy's home!

DARWELL: (NO INTEREST) Hullo.

ARBUTHNOT: Look what I brought you, Darwell!

DARWELL: A tape recorder!

ARBUTHNOT: Would you believe it? Some jerk guy left it in the store.

DARWELL: A customer?

ARBUTHNOT: No, he didn't make it as a customer. He wanted a ten-cent candy bar, but he only had a nickel.

DARWELL: So he didn't get the candy bar - and he got mad - and went off in a huff and left his tape recorder?

ARBUTHNOT: Something like that. Now it's yours!

DARWELL: Thanks, Dad! (CHANGE) Oh, I forgot to tell you . . . Uncle Julian and Aunt Bernice got here. They're out in the patio with Mom.

DUNKLE: So the company stayed for a week. Mr. Arbuthnot and his little family entertained them and when there were about to leave, Uncle Julian said to Darwell:

JULIAN: Darwell, you've got a splendid tape recorder there. If

	you'll dictate a letter on tape into it and send it to Aunt Bernice and me . . . after we returned to Nebraska . . . we'll send you a dandy present!! Will you do that?
DARWELL:	Sure, I will! I wanna use my new tape recorder anyway!!
DUNKLE:	So after the relatives had gone . . . and had enough time to get home . . . Darwell picked up the microphone and dictated a letter to Uncle Julian and Aunt Bernice.
DARWELL:	(READS) Dear Uncle Julian and Aunt Bernice . . . We all certainly enjoyed your visit. The time just flew, as Mama said. Dad enjoyed hearing about your work in the grain elevator business . . . and was deeply concerned about your foot trouble. (FADE) We hated to see you go back to Omaha . . .
DUNKLE:	Now that's what Darwell dictated on the tape recorder . . . but because of the magical interference of Al A. Kazam, who was mad about not getting his candy bar . . . this is what Uncle Julian and Aunt Bernice heard when they received the tape in Omaha.
DARWELL:	(FADE IN) Dumb Uncle Julian and Aunt Bernice . . . The week you were with us was a big drag! Seemed more like a year . . . trying to figure out something to entertain a couple of hicks like you. My father wanted to play in his yearly golf tournament . . . and prune his roses . . . but instead, he had to sit around with a splitting headache, listening to your silly anecdotes about your ole grain elevator . . . and how your corns were

killing you. Who cares! What a relief, having you back in Nebraska. Just stay there! Your bored-stiff nephew, Darwell. Drop dead already!!

DONNIE: Wow! That was some letter!

DUNKLE: Just the opposite of what Darwell had really said. The evil magician saw to that! Well, Uncle Julian blew his stack and Aunt Bernice had fits. They wrote to Darwell's parents and told them of the recorded letter they'd received. When Darwell heard about it - he was really shocked, because he loved his Uncle Julian and Aunt Bernice! And, of course, he never did get that dandy present Uncle Julian had promised.

DONNIE: Was it really dandy?

DUNKLE: Um.

DONNIE: Tough!

DUNKLE: And then, do you know what happened?

DONNIE: No . . . Do you?

DUNKLE: Sure. Mr. Arbuthnot realized how the tape recorder was enchanted . . . and what a 'put on' it was. It seemed obvious to him now . . . that whatever was spoken into the tape recorder, the opposite in meaning was recorded! Darwell wouldn't have anything to do with the tape recorder, so Arnold and Martha, his wife, experimented. She would say 'I love you, Arnold' . . . and on the playback, what they heard was 'I hate you, Arnold' - just the opposite! So Arnold took the tape recorder back to the store . . . and he noticed once again, the brass-plate which read: 'The last recording on this machine will come true.' So Arnold fired it up and recorded something . . . and then he put it down behind the counter. (BEAT) Three days later, the roly-poly magician came in once more.

SOUND: DOOR OPENED – BELL TINKLE – DOOR CLOSED

KAZAM: Hi! I'm back! (GIGGLE) Remember me? (GIGGLE) Been doing any recording lately?

ARBUTHNOT: On the tape recorder you left? Yes.

KAZAM: Are you sorry now that you didn't sell me a candy bar for a nickel?

ARBUTHNOT: In a way.

KAZAM: You've been doing a little recording, huh?

ARBUTHNOT: Um.

KAZAM: You got any friends left? (GIGGLE) You notice the brass-plate?

ARBUTHNOT: Um.

KAZAM: The last recorded request will come true! You're aware of that?

ARBUTHNOT: Um.

KAZAM: Lemme hear what you recorded!

DUNKLE: Now, of course, what Arnold had recorded was . . .

ARBUTHNOT: I don't need you - or anything you can give me. I don't want and would refuse, if you gave it to me, one million dollars minus five cents!

DUNKLE: . . .so when Arnold played the tape back, this is what came out . . .

ARBUTHNOT: I do need you and I want what you can give me. I want and would not refuse one million dollars plus five cents!

KAZAM: Betrayed! Betrayed! (GIGGLE) You used the gimmick!

ARBUTHNOT: Wasn't it an obvious ploy? Didn't take any great intelligence to figure out. Will I get the million dollars plus five cents?

KAZAM: Of course you'll get it! I'm an evil musician . . . uh . . . magician . . . I never said I was smart. I knew I hadn't worked out the magic formula right . . . and I was gonna get back to it, but I never did. I'm evil . . . and stupid . . . but I'm honest! Will you take this certified check for a million dollars?

ARBUTHNOT: I will.

KAZAM: I now pronounce you a very rich dude! (GIGGLE)

ARBUTHNOT: I appreciate it. You're not such an evil magician . . . at least I don't think so.

KAZAM: But you do think I'm stupid.

ARBUTHNOT: Oh sure . . . I think you're stupid. I'm glad you're stupid. (AWKWARD PAUSE) Well, I guess that takes care of things. Why're you just standing there?

KAZAM: Would you add your five cents to my five cents and let me have that ten-cent candy bar?

ARBUTHNOT: Why not?

DUNKLE: So Al A. Kazam got his candy bar and Arnold got a million dollars. (UP) Why are you crinkling up your forehead, Donnie?

DONNIE: I was just thinking . . . if Arnold Arbuthnot had given Al A. Kazam the candy bar for five cents in the beginning . . . none of this would have happened.

DUNKLE: I'll tell you that story next time . . . it just won't take as long.

"THE FLYING TURTLE"

DUNKLE: (LAFF)

DONNIE: Whatta ya laughin' at, Uncle Dunkle.

DUNKLE: (LAFF) Well, Donnie - I was just thinkin' about a lil turtle who wanted wings and what happened to him when he tried to fly!

DONNIE: Turtles can't fly!

DUNKLE: Well, that's true of most turtles . . . but Teddy . . . well, just listen. It all started one day when lil Teddy turtle's mother said:

MAMA: Teddy, I want you to go to the store and bring home a nice, big plate of hot soup for your papa's lunch.

TEDDY:	Yes, mama. I'll hurry as fast as I can!
DUNKLE:	But everybody knows that turtles just can't hurry very fast . . . so, pretty soon, Teddy turtle though to himself:
TEDDY:	If I had nice, long legs - like a rabbit - I could do all my errands real fast! . . . and have lot's of time to play!
DUNKLE:	. . . and then Teddy got a wonderful idea! On his way to the store, in stopped in the woods to see sleepy ol' Mr. Toad, the magician . . .
MR. TOAD:	SNORES - CONTINUES UNDER:
TEDDY:	Mr. Toad? (BEAT) Mr. Toad? Please wake up!
MR. TOAD:	(WAKES UP) Uh? What? Huh? Oh, hello, Teddy turtle. What can I do for you?
TEDDY:	Mr. Toad, I'm tired of my lil ol' short legs! I'd like to have long legs - like a rabbit!
MR. TOAD:	Oh? Hmm. Well . . . uh . . . Teddy . . . (LAYS IT OUT) A turtle's a turtle . . . and a rabbit's a rabbit. I'm not sure you'd like long legs . . . if ya had them.
TEDDY:	Oh yes, I would, Mr. Toad! Really, I would!
MR. TOAD:	Well . . . we'll see. (BEAT) Go over to that wishin' pond . . . over there . . . Turn around three times . . .
SOUND:	SPLASHING WATER
	. . .that's it . . . (BEAT) Now, look what you have.
TEDDY:	My legs! They're long!! Oh, thank you, Mr. Toad!! You're a wonderful magician!!

DUNKLE:	Then, Teddy tried out his new long legs by runnin' outta the forest as fast as he could run. He ran all the way to the store and bought a nice plate of hot soup. Then, he started home . . . when, all of a sudden, he saw . . . a rabbit.
TEDDY:	Hello, Willy rabbit!
WILLY:	(DOWN) Hello, Teddy turtle. (UP) Teddy! Where did you get those long legs? They're almost like mine!
TEDDY:	Almost? They *are* like yours! (THINKS) Say, Willy! How about a race? Even when I'm carrying this plate of soup, I can run faster than *you*!
WILLY:	You think so? Well, we'll see about that! Ready! Set! Go!
DUNKLE:	So Teddy turtle ran a race with Willy Rabbit . . . but just then, a crow flew down to see the fun . . .
CROW:	CAW-CAW-CAW!
DUNKLE:	. . .and when Teddy looked up at the crow . . . he tripped over a stone . . . fell down . . . and the plate of hot soup spilled . . . all over him! (CHANGE) Well, there was Teddy turtle - with his shell all sticky and the soup in his eyes . . . Now, Donnie, isn't that the funniest thing you ever heard?
DONNIE:	It sure is, Uncle Dunkle . . . only you said Teddy turtle could fly . . .
DUNKLE:	Well, wait, Donnie, I'm not finished with the story. Teddy was a lil fella with big ideas . . . so he got another

plate of hot soup from the store . . . and then, he went back to ol' Mr. Toad, the magician . . .

MR. TOAD: SNORES - CONTINUES UNDER:

TEDDY: Mr. Toad? (BEAT) Mr. Toad? Please wake up!

MR. TOAD: (WAKES UP) Uh? What? Huh? Oh, it's you, Teddy turtle. What's the matter now?

TEDDY: I don't like this big ol' rabbit legs, Mr. Toad! They're so long . . . I can't run on them without falling down!

MR. TOAD: Didn't I tell ya, Teddy?

TEDDY: But . . . birds never trip and fall down! Please, can I have wings - like Mr. Crow?

MR. TOAD: Wings, eh? (LAYS IT OUT) Well, Teddy, a turtle's a turtle and a bird is a bird . . . Birds don't weight much, y'know. That's why they can fly - but you're pretty heavy to go up in the air.

TEDDY: Please! Won't you let me try? I just know I can do it!

MR. TOAD: Well . . . alright . . . go over to the wishin' pond and turn around three times.

SOUND: SPLASHING WATER

That's it. (BEAT) Now, look what you have?

TEDDY: I've got my short legs back! . . . and I've got wings! . . . just like a crow! Oh, thank you, Mr. Toad!

DUNKLE: Then, Teddy turtle flapped his brand-new black wings and started to fly! It was hard work but he went higher and higher . . .

TEDDY: I'm flying! I'm flying!

DUNKLE: Yes, Teddy the turtle was flyin' high above the woods! Then, Mr. Crow flew toward him . . .

CROW: CAW-CAW-CAW! Say, aren't you Teddy turtle?

TEDDY: Yes, Mr. Crow! Look at me! I've got wings . . . just like yours!

CROW: CAW-CAW-CAW! So you have! But . . . you're too heavy to stay up here very long. You better go back down on the ground before you fall and hurt yourself.

TEDDY: Oh no! I won't fall! Look! I can even go <u>higher!!</u>

DUNKLE: But the wise ol' owl was right . . . Pretty soon, Teddy's wings began to get tired . . . and he started to go down . . .

TEDDY: I'm too heavy for my wings! I'm falling! I'm falling! Help! Heeeeeeeelp!!

SOUND: LOUD CRASH

DUNKLE: . . . and where do you think Teddy turtle landed, Donnie?

DONNIE: I dunno, Uncle Dunkle? Where?

DUNKLE: Why, right in that new plate of hot soup!

DONNIE: Figures.

DUNKLE: Well, he was so sticky, he had to jump in the wishin' pond for a bath . . .

SOUND: SPLASHING WATER

TEDDY: Mr. Toad? Mr. Toad! My wings are gone!

MR. TOAD: Yes, Teddy . . . you're just a turtle again.

TEDDY: That's all I wanna be! Just a turtle! . . . and I'll never wish for anything foolish again!

DONNIE: That sure is a funny story, Uncle Dunkle . . . Did Teddy's papa ever get his lunch?

DUNKLE: Well, Donnie, Teddy turtle got a new plate of soup for his father's lunch . . . but what do ya know? When he finally got home . . . it was time for supper! (LAFFS)

"THE GREEN COW"

DUNKLE: My name, as you know, is Uncle Dunkle. My nephew is Donnie - and if I'm not mistaken, I think I see him comin' up the path. Yep (CHUCKLE) that's him!!

DONNIE: (OFF) Hi, Uncle Dunkle!!

DUNKLE: Oh, hi, how ya doin'? Come on over here. I want to introduce you formally. (DOWN) I know that they all know who you are and all that, but (CHUCKLE) I feel kinda silly today, so go along with me. O.K.?

DONNIE: O.K.

DUNKLE: Say 'hello' Donnie.

DONNIE: Hello, Donnie!

DUNKLE: No, no, no - just . . . just 'hello!'

DONNIE: Hello.

DUNKLE: Now then, Donnie, I suppose you wonder why I've called you over here today. Well, somethin' has been troublin' me. Uh, this! In the many stories that I've told you . . . uh . . . there have been instances where the animals talked - right?

DONNIE: Yes, there have been such instances, Uncle Dunkle.

DUNKLE: But . . . uh . . . level with me now, Donnie . . . uh . . . you don't believe that the animals really talked, do ya?

DONNIE' Well, I just assumed that you were makin' all that stuff up.

DUNKLE: In point of fact, I was - so today, I'm not gonna tell ya about a talkin' animal - today, I'm gonna tell ya a real sensible story.

DONNIE: What're you gonna tell me about today?

DUNKLE: A green cow.

DONNIE: A green cow?

DUNKLE: Now this particular green cow lived on the . . . uh . . . roof.

DONNIE: Uncle Dunkle, in all my research into the world of cows, I have never heard about a green cow that lived on the roof!

DUNKLE: Well, (CLEARS THROAT) you're young, Donnie - you're . . . uh . . . young.

DONNIE: (DEPRECATINGLY) Oh, yeah! I keep forgettin'!

DUNKLE: At any rate, this particular cow lived on the roof . . .

DONNIE: (UP) Green cow!

DUNKLE: Yeah, that's right - uh, well, her name was . . . uh . . . her name was Effie - and the reason that she lived on the roof was because . . . uh . . . well, she . . . uh . . .

DONNIE: Yeah?

DUNKLE: She . . . uh . . . she happened to like roofs . . . (NERVOUS CHUCKLE) . . . that's all! DONNIE: Uncle Dunkle?

DUNKLE: Yeah, Donnie?

DONNIE: How did she get up . . . on the roof?

DUNKLE: Well, she . . . uh . . . well, that's easy enough to . . . explain. She . . . uh . . . (UP) How did she get up on the roof, did you say?

DONNIE: Uh-huh.

DUNKLE: Oh, yeah - well, she went to bed in the middle of the night, when everybody was asleep . . . and . . . uh . . .

DONNIE: Yeah?

DUNKLE: . . . and . . . uh . . . she . . . got up in the mornin' . . . uh . . . before anybody else did, so . . . actually, nobody knew exactly how she did get up on the roof.

DONNIE: Ummm - I'll accept that.

DUNKLE: Well, one night when she was asleep, a couple of boys threw a pair of shoes at her.

DONNIE: To wake her up, right?

DUNKLE: Right - but Effie was a sound sleeper - so the boys didn't succeed with their little joke. The next mornin' when Effie, the cow . . .

DONNIE: The green cow!

DUNKLE: . . . uh . . . the green cow woke up - there were the two shoes layin' right beside her.

DONNIE: So . . . what'd Effie do?

DUNKLE: I'll tell ya - Effie put those shoes right on her hind feet - and when she got down on the ground, she walked on her front feet.

DONNIE: A cow, walkin' on her front feet?

DUNKLE: A green cow, walkin' on her front feet! Y'see, she figgered that, in this way, she wouldn't wear out her new shoes.

DONNIE: Oh.

DUNKLE: Well, everyday, this green cow - this Effie - she had to go to the store for the farmer - and on this particular day, she walked . . . all the way . . . three miles - on her front feet. When she got to the store, she bought all sorts of things - and the grocery man put 'em in a bag for her. Then Effie stood on her front feet, and the man placed the bag of groceries on her hind feet - and she walked

	home on her front feet, balancin' the nag on her hind feet!
DONNIE:	Question! When she got home, how'd she get the bag down without . . .spillin' everything?
DUNKLE:	Easiest thing in the world! She just tossed the bag up in the air with her hind feet and then stood up real quick and caught the bag with her front feet as it came down! Everyday, she went to the store for the farmer and his wife . . . all summer long - and do you know what they did to reward her, Donnie?
DONNIE:	Sure! When winter came, they put her on a plane and sent her on a trip to California, and she had a fine time, swimmin', fishin' . . .
DUNKLE:	She . . . she . . . she did? (CHUCKLE) Aw, c'mon! You knew all the time I was joshin' you about Effie, didn't ya? (LAFF)
DONNIE:	Sure, Uncle Dunkle - I like the green cow, only . . .
DUNKLE:	Only what?
DONNIE:	Only . . . she wasn't really green, was she?
DUNKLE:	Goodness sakes, no, Donnie! (LAFFS) She was really . . . purple!!

"THE LONESOME UMBRELLA"

DONNIE: (COMING ON) Uncle Dunkle? I'm here for today's story! (BEAT) Uncle Dunkle? Are ya home?

DUNKLE: (COMING ON) Afternoon, Donnie!

DONNIE: Hi, Uncle Dunkle! I thought you left me all alone!

DUNKLE: Now would I do that to my favorite lil nephew?

DONNIE: Well . . . I dunno . . . I guess not . . . it's jus' that . . . it's been happenin' to me a lot . . . lately.

DUNKLE: W-whatta ya mean?

DONNIE: Nothin'.

DUNKLE: You lose a couple o' friends at school?

DONNIE: Sort of . . .

DUNKLE: Have a fight?

DONNIE: Not really. (SIGH) We were all great friends . . . the best . . . last year. Then, we split up for the summer. You know how it is.

DUNKLE: I know.

DONNIE: Usually, when school starts again, we all jus' become pals . . . like we never left each other. But this time, they all got put in the same class together! They all did . . . but I didn't!

DUNKLE: And now they're ignorin' you.

DONNIE: Exactly.

DUNKLE: Y'know, Donnie, bein' lonesome isn't very pleasant . . .

DONNIE: Yer tellin' me.

DUNKLE: But you're jist goin' through a phase . . . Even I get lonesome . . . once in a while. That doesn't mean I'm not needed . . . It jist means others haven't seen what a nice fella I am . . . but sooner or later . . . if they're friends worth havin' . . . they come around!

DONNIE: What if nobody likes me'?

DUNKLE: Donnie! A swell fella like you'? Not be liked! I'm flabbergasted! In fact, my <u>flabber</u> has never been so <u>gasted</u>!! (CHANGE) Why, you're a very likable little fellow! But even someone who's well liked can still be lonesome.

Now, I'm gonna tell you a story about a lonesome umbrella that nobody wanted.

DONNIE: Gosh, Uncle Dunkle, everybody likes umbrellas for when it rains . . . I like my umbrella!

DUNKLE: Sure you do, Donnie . . . and lots o' people like their umbrellas. I suppose the one I'm gonna tell you about would have been very contented and happy if . . . and it's a big 'if' . . . it had ever rained. Umbrellas dearly love the rain, y'know.

DONNIE: I know.

DUNKLE: But the only time anybody ever takes an umbrella out for a walk is when it does rain. As long as the sun's shinin', umbrellas stay in the house!

DONNIE: Did you say it <u>never</u> rained, Uncle Dunkle?

DUNKLE: It never rained where the umbrella lived. This umbrella lived on the desert.

DONNIE: Doesn't it rain on the desert?

DUNKLE: Nope! No sir! Sun shines nearly all the time. (BEAT) Well, one day the umbrella was talkin' to a cane he lived with in the closet . . .

UMBRELLA: Mr. Cane?

CANE: (QUIET, SELF-ASSURED) Yes, Mr. Umbrella?

UMBRELLA: (UNSURE) May I talk with you, Mr. Cane?

CANE: (CLEARS THROAT) I suppose so. Be brief. I do have an appointment, shortly.

"The Lonesome Umbrella" 205

UMBRELLA: I know. I know! (BEAT) Mr. Cane . . . I wish I were you. You go for a walk every day with Uncle Charlie.

CANE: (BORED) Yes . . . he's got a sore foot. Sometimes, it gets a bit tiresome . . . Some day, I'd just like to take it easy.

UMBRELLA: And I'd give anything if somebody'd take me out. I stay in this old, gloomy closet all the time . . . and I'm soooo lonesome.

CANE: Yes, this is fascinating, Mr. Umbrella . . . But I do have other things to do.

UMBRELLA: But Mr. Cane! (UP) Oh, here comes Uncle Charlie now!!

CANE: (BORED) Yes, I know.

UMBRELLA: Maybe he'll take me out for a walk today.

CANE: Not likely.

UMBRELLA: I wish he would.

CHARLIE: (COMING ON) My cane! Where's my cane`? Where'd I put it? . . . Oh, here it is . . . in the closet.

CANE: Where he always puts me.

UMBRELLA: He's forgetful sometimes.

CANE: (MEAN) Yes, he forgot all about <u>you</u>.

CHARLIE: (UP) John! I'm goin' fer a walk now!

JOHN: (OFF) See ya later, Uncle Charlie!!

UMBRELLA: Goodbye, Mr. Cane... have a nice time.

CANE: I'll try, but I doubt it... these daily walks are so boring!

UMBRELLA: (TO HIMSELF) They wouldn't be to me! (SIGH) I'm so lonesome!! I wish someone would just... dust me once in a while. It would show they cared... a little.

DONNIE: Gee, Mr. Umbrella really was all alone! He's got it way, way worse off than me!

DUNKLE: Whatta ya mean'?

DONNIE: He didn't have anybody in the whole-wide world...

DUNKLE: Yeah.

DONNIE: At least, I have you, Uncle Dunkle!

DUNKLE: (LAFF) Thanks, Donnie.

DONNIE: Don't mention it.

DUNKLE: You have Aunt Rapunzel, too! Don't forget her.

DONNIE: Where is Aunt Rapunzel?

DUNKLE: She's sittin' in the closet.

DONNIE: What's she doin' in there?

DUNKLE: She's dustin' her umbrella... so he won't get all lonesome... like the one in the story.

DONNIE: She is not!

DUNKLE: Well, she's doin' somethin'...

DONNIE: So tell me more about the umbrella in the story! What happened to him?

DUNKLE: Well, one day, when the umbrella was lonesomer than he'd ever been before, Mr. Cane up and said:

CANE: Uncle Charlie is going away. He's moving out to California.

UMBRELLA: He . . . He is!

CANE: Yes. I'll be going along . . . naturally.

UMBRELLA: Naturally. (SIGH)

CANE: His sore foot, y'know.

UMBRELLA: I know. (SIGH)

CANE: He needs me.

UMBRELLA: You sure are lucky, Mr. Cane.

DUNKLE: So there was a lot of excitement around the house, Donnie . . . and finally, the day came when Uncle Charlie was to leave for California.

CHARLIE: John, you take care now . . . I'll write you when I get to Californy.

JOHN: Say, Uncle Charlie, you're gonna take the umbrella, aren't ya?

CHARLIE: Why, I hadn't thought about it, John. Whatever fer?

JOHN: It rains in Californy . . . up north where yer goin', 'specially!

CHARLIE: Huh! That's right, by gum! I forgot there was such a thing as rain: (LAFF)

UMBRELLA: (BRIGHT) Did you hear that, Mr. Cane?

CANE: (DOWN) Yes, you're coming along. I hope there's enough room in the new closet for both of us.

JOHN: Uncle Charlie, what'd the doc say about yer sore foot?

CHARLIE: He said I won't have to use the cane anymore!

CANE: (UP) Oh, dear! This is dreadful news!!

CHARLIE: I'll leave the cane here, John . . . and take the umbrella . . . then, if my foot should bother me again, I can use it for a cane . . . and I can also use it when it rains.

SOUND: DOUBLE TOOT OF TAXI

CHARLIE: Well, there's my cab. G'bye, John!

JOHN: So-long, Uncle Charlie!

UMBRELLA: (CALLS) Oh, Mr. Cane! He's tucking me under his arm! I'm going out into the great, wide world at last!!

CANE: (WORRIED) Yes . . . and I'll have to stay in this old musty, gloomy closet all the time!!

UMBRELLA: Well, Mr. Cane . . . you did say that someday you'd like to take it easy. (UP) California! Here I come!!

DUNKLE: . . . and the lonesome umbrella was no longer . . . lonesome!!

DONNIE: Gosh! Uncle Dunkle, I liked the story of the lonesome umbrella!

DUNKLE: Glad ya did!

DONNIE: And I'll never take OUR time together for granted . . . the way Mr. Cane did to Uncle Charlie!

DUNKLE: I enjoy our time t'gether too, Donnie.

DONNIE: (BRIGHT) You do?!

DUNKLE: Sure. (BRIGHT) Who else am I gonna get to sit and listen to my stories?

DONNIE: That's true.

"THE MAGIC DRUMS"

SOUND: (OFF) DRUM ROLLS - CYMBAL CRASHES - "HIGH-HAT" - HELD UNDER:

DUNKLE: (CHUCKLES) My nephew, Donnie, sure enjoys that set of drums I bought him . . . and to show his appreciation, he plays 'em <u>all the time</u>! (SIGHS) Oh, he takes time out to eat his lunch and then back he goes! Sometimes I wish he didn't appreciate 'em <u>so much</u>!

SOUND: DRUMS ARE PLAYED LOUDER - SUSTAIN:

DUNKLE: He's gettin' good at 'em, too! Too good! (CALLS) Say, Donnie!

SOUND:	DRUMS OUT
DONNIE:	Yeah, Uncle Dunkle?
DUNKLE:	I wanna take me a little snooze, so hold it down on those 'skins' - as you call 'em, O.K?
DONNIE:	O.K . . . I'll think about doin' my history homework.
DUNKLE:	Instead of '<u>thinkin</u>' about doin' it - <u>I think</u> you better do it.
DONNIE:	I will, Uncle Dunkle. But for a few minutes, I think I'll just play my good-ole-drums a little bit more. I'll play 'em soft like.
DUNKLE:	Soft! Can't be done! That's like jumpin' in the pool and only gettin' damp!
DONNIE:	(GIGGLES)
SOUND:	DRUMS START
DUNKLE:	(YAWNS) Oh, I'm sleepy. I better just set the alarm clock so I don't snooze too long.
SOUND:	WINDING ALARM CLOCK
DUNKLE:	(VOICE GRADUALLY FADES AWAY) I'm so sleepy . . . (YAWN) Oh, this couch feels <u>soooo good</u>! (YAWN)
SOUND:	HARP GLISS COMES IN AS UNCLE DUNKLE'S VOICE FADES AWAY (GOES OUT) AND UNCLE DUNKLE'S VOICE GRADUALLY COMES UP FULL.
DUNKLE:	(FADES ON) I hope Donnie didn't think I was mean but I just don't think he should play those drums <u>all</u> the time. Fun's fun, but . . . (CALLS) Donnie!

DONNIE: (COMES ON) Yeah, Uncle Dunkle?

DUNKLE: I hope I didn't hurt your feelin's about sayin' the drums were too loud . . .

DONNIE: It's O.K.

DUNKLE: It's just that . . . if you play the drums all the time, you'll neglect your history quiz I was gonna help you with. They are dandy drums, I'll have to admit.

DONNIE: Didja know they were "ma . . .

DUNKLE: (GOES ON) You just gotta forget 'em for a while.

DONNIE: Didja know they were "ma . . .

DUNKLE: (GOES ON) You gotta remember your homework.

DONNIE: I'll try, Uncle Dunkle . . . but even when I'm not even sittin' by my drums . . . <u>if anything reminds me of drums</u> . . . d'ya know what happens?

DUNKLE: What happens?

DONNIE: You won't believe me.

DUNKLE: Try me.

DONNIE: (UNCERTAIN) Well . . . (BLURTS IT OUT) if anything reminds me of drums . . .

DUNKLE: . . .go on . . .

DONNIE: (QUICKLY) They start to play <u>all by themselves</u>!!

DUNKLE: . . .all by . . . <u>themselves</u>?

DONNIE: Yeah, like I was tryin' to tell ya - they're "Magic Drums!!"

DUNKLE: Magic?

DONNIE: That's what it said on the box.

DUNKLE: I didn't see that.

DONNIE: 'course not! They wrapped it in pretty paper when you got 'em at the store - but I'm the one who took the pretty paper off - and I saw what it said . . .

DUNKLE: Magic drums!

DONNIE: Magic drums . . . and like I said, if anything reminds me of drum stuff, they start to play themselves.

DUNKLE: I got to get your mind off drums. (UP) I know! I'll tell you a nursery rhyme! You still like those?

DONNIE: Oh, sure!

DUNKLE: Here's one! Little Bo Poop, fell in the soup, but don't just stand and stare, I have no doubt they'll fish her out . . . with noodles in her hair!! (LAFF)

DONNIE: (GIGGLES) Oh, you made that one up! Tell me an old one!

DUNKLE: There was one about <u>the piper's son</u> . . . let's see . . . how'd it go . . .

DONNIE: Tom-tom.

SOUND: TWO LICKS ON THE TOM-TOM

DONNIE: Uh . . . tom-tom.

SOUND: TWO MORE LICKS ON THE TOM-TOM

DONNIE: I forgot. Tom-tom . . .

SOUND: TWO LICKS ON TOM-TOM

DONNIE: . . .is what one of my drums is called!

DUNKLE: (STRESSES) Tom-tom, the 'piper's son' - it's a different kind of Tom-tom! (STERN) Knock it off, you 'magic' drums!!

SOUND: DRUMS STOP

DUNKLE: (SIGHS) Shhheeeeeee!

SOUND: DRUM ROLL STARTS AGAIN

DUNKLE: (UP) I said . . . desist!!

SOUND: DRUM TRAILS OFF AND STOPS

DUNKLE: That's better.

SOUND: THREE QUICK BEATS

DUNKLE: We have got us a real problem here, Donnie. (UNDER HIS BREATH) Smart-aleck drums! (UP) We gotta get our minds on somethin' else, Donnie . . .

DONNIE: . . .like what, Uncle Dunkle?

DUNKLE: Well, I thought it'd be kinda nice, while we're sittin' outside here on the patio . . . to have a second breakfast.

DONNIE: Sounds groovy!

DUNKLE: I thought maybe some chocolate milk and . . .

DONNIE: (QUICKLY) Don't say it!!

DUNKLE: Rolls!

SOUND: DRUM ROLL STARTS - HOLD UNDER:

DUNKLE: . . .don't say <u>what</u>?

DONNIE: You <u>already</u> said it. 'Rolls' reminded me of my drums.

DUNKLE: Drum rolls . . . that's right!

SOUND: DRUM ROLLS CONTINUE STRONGER - UNDER:

DUNKLE: I meant <u>cinnamon</u> rolls, you goofy drum! Now pay <u>attention</u>!

SOUND: DRUM STOPS

DUNKLE: They're magic drums, sure enough! Well, let's not think about drum things anymore . . . let's think about your history quiz! (LOOKS) I'll just look at these questions I wrote down . . . (UP) Here's one! <u>What</u> is the eagle to the United States?

DONNIE: (THINKS) Uh . . . it's a . . . it's a . . . <u>symbol</u>!!

SOUND: FOUR CYMBAL CRASHES

(ANNOYED) Hey, drums! Can't you spell?

SOUND: SINGLE CYMBAL CRASH

Not cymbal! The symbol I mean . . .

SOUND: SINGLE CYMBAL CRASH

. . .is spelled . . . symbol!

SOUND: LOW RUMBLING ROLL

(UP) QUIET!

SOUND: DRUM OUT

Thanks a heap.

SOUND:	SINGLE INSOLENT THUMP
DONNIE:	(DISGUSTED) Oh, it's no use, Uncle Dunkle . . . everything reminds me of my drums . . .
DUNKLE:	We'll just have to be more careful. (CHANGE) Gettin' back to our history quiz . . . What kind of hat does Uncle Sam wear?
DONNIE:	I can't tell ya, Uncle Dunkle.
DUNKLE:	You mean, you 'don't know'!
DONNIE:	No, it's just that it's somethin' about a drum too!
DUNKLE:	Nonsense! Just tell me . . . what kind of hat does Uncle Sam wear?
DONNIE:	Well, you asked for it! (QUICKLY) A high-hat!!
SOUND:	DRUM MAKES SOUND OF A TOP-HAT - HOLDS UNDER:
DONNIE:	That's what a 'high-hat' sounds like.
SOUND:	MORE INSISTENT HIGH-HAT LICKS
DUNKLE:	Too loud! That's enough to make us jump out of our skins!
SOUND:	ALL PARTS OF THE DRUM SET GO WILD–HOLD UNDER:
DONNIE:	Uncle Dunkle, 'Skins' is another name for a drum-set.
SOUND:	DRUMS CONTINUE TO GO WILD - BUT FINALLY TAPER OFF AND FADE – AS ALARM CLOCK BELL GOES OFF. (DRUMS NOW OUT COMPLETELY)
DUNKLE:	(WAKES UP - FIGHTING SLEEP) Oh, those pesky drums!

They've taken over! . . . they've . . . they've (PAUSE - AND THEN) Wait a minute! I don't hear the drums anymore!! Strange! (REACTS) . . . and what am I doin' here on the couch? (REMEMBERS) Oh, sure! I remember now. I took me a little snooze. I was sound asleep . . . and I must have been dreamin' (CALLS) Hey, Donnie! C'mere! Have I got a dream to tell you about.

"THE TALKING VIOLIN"

DUNKLE: I think I already know the answer to this, Donnie - so the question is actually academic.

DONNIE: That means you don't hafta ask it?

DUNKLE: Yeah, you could say that - but just to be sure, I'll go ahead and ask it.

DONNIE: So ask it.

DUNKLE: Do you like music?

DONNIE: Sure! You know I do.

DUNKLE: Well, I know you like 'somethin'! (CHUCKLE)

DONNIE:	Oh, come on, Uncle Dunkle! You jus' don't understand the kinda music I like.
DUNKLE:	That's not entirely true. I'll go along with you on your kind of music cuz I think some of it is O.K. I like it myself.
DONNIE:	(MIFFED) Thanks a bunch!
DUNKLE:	Some of it I like a lot.
DONNIE:	How much?
DUNKLE:	A little! (CHUCKLE) I'm jus' teasin' you, Donnie. The important thing about musical appreciation is that you're the best judge of what you honestly enjoy. You like what you like - when you get as old as I am, you may like something else.
DONNIE:	If I can still hear it.
DUNKLE:	Huh?
DONNIE:	I said, 'if I can still hear it!'
DUNKLE:	I heard ya.
DONNIE:	You should, I gave you two chances.
DUNKLE:	(CHUCKLE) Guess you did at that!
DONNIE:	Is the lecture over?
DUNKLE:	All over.
DONNIE:	Then how about the music story?
DUNKLE:	Good idea! (CLEARS THROAT)
DONNIE:	(INTERRUPTS) Oh Uncle Dunkle . . . before you get started, d'ya think Aunt Rapunzel would like to hear the story too?

DUNKLE: She's busy. DONNIE: Doin' what?

DUNKLE: She's out back – teachin' a pigeon how to walk people-toed.

DONNIE: (IMPRESSED) Wow! (TAKE) Oh, she is not!

DUNKLE: Well, she's doin' somethin'.

DONNIE: O.K. - on with the story!

DUNKLE: It's all about a violin . . . an old violin . . . and a little girl named Patty.

DONNIE: Was it Patty's violin?

DUNKLE: It was indeed.

DONNIE: . . .and did Patty like music and playing her violin?

DUNKLE: She liked music well enough - she liked to listen to it – but she didn't like practicin'. She got impatient when she didn't play the notes right off - an' she'd get downright discouraged and she'd say:

PATTY: It's no use! I'll never learn to play this old violin! I can't remember even <u>one</u> of the five positions - and when I hold the bow, it slips! And when I do try to play, the ugly old thing squeaks! I just won't ever be able to play it!

VIOLIN: (UP) Hey! Watch you mouth! I'm not ugly - I still gotta skin like a bambino!!

DONNIE: Did Patty hear him say that?

DUNKLE: No, because he was speaking very softly - to himself, really. The old violin used to worry about Patty's deprecatory self-evaluation . . .

DONNIE: (UP) . . . and that she couldn't play good, right?

DUNKLE: That too! The violin was fond of Patty. He was quite old and the patina of his varnish was almost as beautiful as the sounds he could produce . . . and had produced. He understood her impatience and spoke softly to himself again.

VIOLIN: Oh my! I feel so sorry for little Patty! She thinks she will never be able to play . . . like she said: 'this old violin!' That's true! I am old – very old but I come from a famous family. I am a Stradivarius.

DONNIE: What's a "strada-various," Uncle Dunkle?

DUNKLE: It's the name of the man who made it many years ago . . . there are only a few left in the world and they are extremely valuable . . . and then the violin said:

VIOLIN: I am modest . . . and yet I know that I'm a great violin. I am modest only until someone runs a bow across my strings and then I sing! I come to life! I am vibrant and I sing as only a violin can! With glory!

DUNKLE: You see, Donnie - what Patty didn't realize was that playing any violin - old or new - was difficult - and took many hours of practice and determination. But something else bothered her too . . . and the old violin knew what it was.

VIOLIN: Patty is unhappy because she doesn't have any young friends. She is lonely. I am not young . . . but I will be her friend!

PATTY: Well, it's that time again. I better get it over with and practice on my dumb old violin.

VIOLIN: (UP) Why does that make you unhappy, Patty?

PATTY:	(GOES ON) It isn't any fun and I can't do it right and . . . (TAKE) My violin! It talked to me!
VIOLIN:	I speak right up. I talk pretty good, huh?
PATTY:	But you're a violin! You can't talk!!
VIOLIN:	Oh, but I can! I talked to you before but you never heard me.
PATTY:	Why not?
VIOLIN:	Because you were angry with me. You made me your enemy . . . but you kept getting lonelier . . . and now that you need a friend so much, you can hear me . . . because I am gonna be your true friend and help you!
PATTY:	I can't believe what's happening!
VIOLIN:	Believe it! Believe me! I will help you and I always keep my word!
PATTY:	Help me . . . how?
VIOLIN:	I tell you how . . . is <u>easy</u>! First, you put me in my case and we go for a stroll . . . or maybe is better to take the bus if I get too heavy.
PATTY:	Where do you wanna go, violin?
VIOLIN:	Just call me 'Stradie!' . . . Where we will go is the concert hall.
PATTY:	Why?
VIOLIN:	Because the world's great violinist, Simon Doring, is rehearsing for a concert there!

"The Talking Violin"   223

DUNKLE: So Patty put Stradie in his case - and off they went to the concert hall. When they arrived the violin said:

VIOLIN: Look around you, Patty! I love the concert hall - and it feels so good to be back.

PATTY: You were here before?

VIOLIN: Many times! When Simon was a tiny baby . . . I was already very old! Try to imagine, Patty, this concert hall . . . with every seat taken - everyone waiting - being oh so quiet! . . . and then that moment!

PATTY: That moment?

VIOLIN: That moment when they hear the first touch of the bow on my strings! Oh, it was glorious!

DUNKLE: . . .and then Simon Doring walked in. He saw Patty and the violin.

VIOLIN: There he is! It's Simon Doring, Patty! Speak to him!

PATTY: I'm embarrassed! What should I say?

VIOLIN: Take me over to him . . . ask him if I'm a good violin!

PATTY: Oh, you <u>know</u> you are, Stradie!!

VIOLIN: Maybe it's what you call my vanity - but it's nice to hear it again!!

PATTY: O.K. I'll do it. (PAUSE) (UP) Mr. Doring!

DORING: Yes? What is it, young lady?

PATTY: My name is Patty - and I wonder if you'd look at my violin.

DORING: Ah, a young musician - it would be my pleasure.

PATTY:	Here he is . . . (UP) I mean, here it is!
DORING:	This is your violin?
PATTY:	Yes.
DUNKLE:	Simon Doring played a short phrase - he smiled at its beauty.
DORING:	Now this is a violin! I'm positive it must be a Stradivarius.
PATTY:	He is . . . I mean, <u>it is!</u> It was willed to me by my Uncle . . . Arnold Kopensky. He was a violinist.
DORING:	. . .and one of the greatest! I took a few lessons from him before he died. You are a fortunate girl!! This is one of the finest instruments in the world!
VIOLIN:	Oh, I am so proud!!
DORING:	Did you say something, Patty?
PATTY:	No sir . . . it was my violin. He . . . <u>it</u> talks to me.
DORING:	What?
PATTY:	Talks to me. (FUSSED) See, Mr. Doring . . . I don't have any friends and I've been lonely . . . so my violin, he . . . <u>it</u> talks to me and now he's my friend. I know that sounds silly!
DORING:	Silly? Nonsense! We must never question a friend - a friend is as rare as talent. Music is the universal language -it speaks to us all - no matter where we're from we can all understand . . . perfectly . . . the beauty of music.
VIOLIN:	That is why you heard me talk to you, Patty . . . because I am beautiful (FLUSTERED) My music, I mean!

PATTY:	(UP) Mr. Doring - would you play something else on my friend . . . uh, mean, my violin?
DORING:	My pleasure!
DUNKLE:	Simon Doring gently placed the violin under his chin and applied the bow. The music was like nothing Patty had ever heard before!
PATTY:	It's heavenly! I wish I could play like that. (ENTHUSED) Oh, Mr. Doring, I'll bet you have lots of friends!
DORING:	Yes, Patty - I do - all over. I've played in all the great cities and wherever I go, I find friends . . . because they like my music, they like me.
PATTY:	I like you.
DORING:	And I like you, Patty. You study your music - learn to play your violin - play beautiful music for people and they'll like you, too. (CHANGE) Oh, and another thing . . . see that she does practice, old violin!
VIOLIN:	Oh, I will! Don' worry about it! I promise! . . . and I never break my word!
DORING:	Good! Now, Patty - you'd better get on home and get busy. You wouldn't want your violin . . . I mean, your friend to break his promise, would you?
PATTY:	I will practice, Mr. Doring - every day. I'm going to be just like <u>you</u>, Mr. Doring!!
DORING:	Oh no you won't, Patty . . . you'll be 'just like you'! Both of us will find our own friends . . . through 'our own' music.

VIOLIN: He talks nice!

DORING: You practice - and see if it doesn't work out that way!

PATTY: Oh, I will, Mr. Doring! I really will!

VIOLIN: Let's go home!

"THE TARDY WEDDING GUEST"

DUNKLE: Hi, Donnie! Well, I see you're right on time for our story.

DONNIE: Oh, I don't like to belate, Uncle Dunkle - and you told me that it's not considerate of your friends . . . or Uncle.

DUNKLE: Well, can't I be your friend . . . and Uncle? (LAFF)

DONNIE: Aw, come on! You know what I mean!

DUNKLE: (LAFF) Yessir, it's important to be on time for all appointments - and especially "special" occasions . . . like weddin's.

DONNIE: I've never been to a wedding.

DUNKLE: The tortoise hadn't either - all he knew was that one morning an invitation came. Miss Hermione Hummingbird was getting married at a place ten miles from where the tortoise lived - which was a long way for a tortoise. He didn't even remember knowin' any humming bird, and as for the weddin' - he didn't want to go, really. He wasn't much on social affairs - he didn't have any small talk - but it would be impolite not to go - so he went to rent a tuxedo.

TORTOISE: I wanna rent a tuxedo.

MAN: A tuxedo. I don't think I got a tuxedo on the rack for a tortoise.

TORTOISE: It could be for a turtle - we're related. You got a tuxedo for a very large turtle? - with a tortoise-neck sweater, maybe?

MAN: I just don't carry tuxedos for animals.

TORTOISE: I'm a reptile.

MAN: Reptile's a snake!

TORTOISE: Huh-uh, nope, no - we're just in the same family, see? Tortoises, turtles, snakes. (UP) If you think I'm hard to fit, (CHUCKLE) how'd you like to fix a snake up with a tuxedo? - no legs!!

MAN: Well, I could just put 'im in an old sleeve.

TORTOISE: I never thought of that! (BEAT) You can't fix me up, eh?

MAN: Say, uh, why don't you try a tortoise tuxedo shop?

TORTOISE: They have those?

MAN: If they don't, you're not gonna get a tuxedo!

TORTOISE: Look, I got a long way to go and I need, desperately, a tuxedo (so I'll look swell, y'know?) Could you just paint me black?

DUNKLE: So the man painted the tortoise black and started out for the wedding. In two years, he'd gone about four miles. He just kept travelin' steadily - and finally, he reached the freeway.

TORTOISE: Look at those cars! They never stop! They keep comin'! Oh! I'll never get across there! I'd better wait 'til night-time - it won't be so busy!!

DUNKLE: So he waited 'til night - but even then, with less traffic, by the time the tortoise would have got to the center of the freeway, a car coming from five miles away would be on top him!!

TORTOISE: It's a good thing that I studied the laws of probabilities at Tortoise Tech, that's all I got to say!! I'd be a fool to go out on that freeway! Pyeh!! No way!!!

DUNKLE: Then, he noticed a mole by the side of the freeway.

TORTOISE: Ja Wohl, Mole! I used that German salutation because it rhymes with mole - and I thought you might find it amusing, and help me out with my plight. I got a real plight, y'know!

MOLE: I'm fairly amused - but I got a heart as big as all underground . . . so what's your plight?

TORTOISE: My plight - or trouble . . .

MOLE: You don't have to explain it. I know what a plight is!

TORTOISE: Look, I gotta go to this hummingbird's wedding, y'see? And it's about six miles away - give or take a foot-and-a-half - and this freeway (LAFF) you wouldn't believe!!

MOLE: Whatta ya want from me? Moles never carry any big bills. Just a characteristic of moles - I haven't got it on me!!

TORTOISE: Perish forbid!! I don't want your money - I want you to burrow a tunnel under the freeway, so I can follow you, real close, and get to the other side! (GIGGLE) Clever, eh?

MOLE: And what do I get out of it?

TORTOISE: Well, I won't eat you for openers!

MOLE: Eat me? You like moles?

TORTOISE: No, but when you're a tortoise, you can get used to anything!!

MOLE: You're kiddin' about eatin' me?

TORTOISE: Of course I am!! I'll pay you for your time and trouble . . . whichever comes first . . . either or - or both!!

MOLE: How much?

TORTOISE: Not how much - how little!! Don't forget, I'm a two-hundred-year-old tortoise! I'm on a pension, which means I have a fixed income! (I gotta watch my pennies, y'know!) How's about diggin' the tunnel under the freeway for me and I'll invite you to the wedding as my guest!! (UP) You ever been to a wedding?

MOLE: No.

TORTOISE: Neither have I! I'll tell you what - let's share this new experience like our new friendship!!

DUNKLE: Well, Donnie, this aimless conversation went on and on and on - for years. And finally, the mole agreed to dig the tunnel - with the tortoise following close along behind him. That took several more years. When they finally reached the other side of the eight-lane freeway, the mole climbed on top of the tortoise and together they continued on their journey to the weddin'. Well, when they finally got there, there was a weddin' gong on all right - but not for Hermione Hummingbird! It was for Hermione Hummingbird's <u>granddaughter</u>!! - but what was worse, they weren't even admitted to the weddin' festivities. As the tortoise explained it:

TORTOISE: Ya wanna know somethin'? I'll tell ya!! I shoulda put on my readin' glasses before I "read" that invitation! It was really addressed to a porpoise! Which makes sense, actually, because I was right - I didn't know any hummingbirds!! (BEAT) Now, if somebody'd just turn me over in the sand, I'll rub off my painted-on tuxedo! (I'm getting' to like it - maybe I'll become a head-waiter - and keep it!!!)

DUNKLE: And that, Donnie, was the story of the tardy wedding guest! (LAFF)

DONNIE: What's so funny, Uncle Dunkle?

DUNKLE: I was just thinkin' (LAFF) Can you imagine how long it would take to get a hamburger (LAFF) if the tortoise was your waiter?!!!

"THEODORE THE TURTLE"

DUNKLE: Well, I guess you're to be congratulated, Donnie. I heard this afternoon that you climbed all the way to the top of Johnson's Hill.

DONNIE: I want to climb to the top of the big pine foothills! That's twice as high . . .!!

DUNKLE: Donnie, you're never satisfied. You remind me of Theodore the turtle. He was never satisfied, either. He was little and he wanted to be big. One day he saw a billboard advertisin' a circus. There was a picture of an elephant and that did it! So he hurried off to the woods to see the wise but always sleepy old Mr. Toad.

TOAD: SNORES

"Theodore the Turtle"

THEODORE: Mr. Toad! Mr. Toad, wake up!

TOAD: (YAWN) What is it, Theodore? You dissatisfied?

THEODORE: Yeah! How can ya tell?

TOAD: Lucky guess. You'd be dissatisfied if you had good health, a million dollars and a wagon with purple wheels . . . and a pink rope to pull it with . . .

THEODORE: You're probably right, Mr. Toad - but this time, I want to be big, big, big like an elephant, because I'm so little that nobody notices me. Everybody looks up to an elephant. (TAKE) Golly! They have to!

TOAD: Let's get it over with! Here's the wishin' pond. Turn around . . . three times, and we'll see what (YAWN)

THEODORE: . . . happens?

TOAD: Happens!

DUNKLE: So Theodore turned around three times and quick as a wink, Theodore was as big as an elephant!

THEODORE: Wow! Thanks, Mr. Toad!!

TOAD: SNORES

THEODORE: He never says "you're welcome."

DUNKLE: Because he was so big, Theodore's legs were longer - and he could walk faster - it didn't take him any time at all to reach the big highway and head for home . . .

BOY: Hey, gang! Look at the big turtle! Looks just like the big pine foot-hills! C'mon, let's climb to the top!

DUNKLE: They jumped up and down and had a fine time - but Theodore didn't enjoy it.

DONNIE: Why not, Uncle Dunkle?

DUNKLE: Well, you see, Donnie - when anybody touches a turtle, they pull their head and tail and legs inside of their shell and with his head inside. Theodore felt just like you would if you got inside of a big church bell when it was ringin'!! (LAFF) He thought he couldn't stand it much longer when luckily the boys decided it was time to go home for supper. Theodore started down the road again. He was passing a restaurant when a man ran out wearin' a cook's apron and a cook's hat . . .

DONNIE: Why, Uncle Dunkle?

DUNKLE: 'cause he was a cook.

DONNIE: Oh.

DUNKLE: . . .and the man said:

MAN: Ooooh! That turtle! It's gigantic! With that turtle, I could make turtle stew for three months! I'll get a rope and tie him up!

DUNKLE: But as soon as the cook ran into the restaurant for a rope, Theodore headed for the river and jumped in! But he wasn't a little feller now - and he didn't sink to the bottom like he used to . . . he stuck way out. The water just came up to the lower part of his shell. He was wonderin' what to do next, when he heard the restaurant man talkin' . . .

MAN:	Where's that big turtle? Where'd he go? Don't see him nowheres! He jus' plumb disappeared (UP) Hmm! Looky that big rock out there in the river. Huh! musta rolled down from the mountainside. I sure would like to know what happened to that turtle!
DUNKLE:	Well, Theodore got out of that predicament - but worse was to come. Theodore was jus' crawlin' out on the riverbank when he heard another man, sort of half-talkin' to hisself:
MAN (2):	Say, this big turtle would make a real nice ferryboat. I could just build a platform on his back for people to stand on and it would be a form of livelihood for me to turn an honest dollar . . .
DONNIE:	. . .and did he, Uncle Dunkle? Did he make a ferryboat out of Theodore?
DUNKLE:	He sure did, Donnie - and charged people twenty-five cents to go across the river. For weeks and weeks, all Theodore did was haul folks across the river - got pretty tiresome, I can tell ya!
DONNIE:	And Theodore could tell me, too!
DUNKLE:	(LAFFS) He'd just about made up his mind that this was what he was gonna do the rest of his live-long life - when he spied the wise but always sleepy old Mr. Toad, sunnin' hisself on a log . . .
THEODORE:	Oh, Mr. Toad - am I overjoyed to see you!!
TOAD:	Who am I talkin' to?

THEODORE: Open your sleepy eyes, Mr. Toad!

TOAD: Oh, good suggestion . . . (UP) Oh, it's Theodore!!

THEODORE: I'd give anything to be little again, Mr. Toad - nobody ever noticed me when I was little.

TOAD: (YAWN) But I thought you wanted to be noticed . . .

THEODORE: Not anymore! Oh, no! Look at all these people on my back. If I could only escape and get back to the wishin' pond! Oh boy!

TOAD: Not much chance of that, Theodore. (LAFF)

THEODORE: I don't see anything to laugh at, Mr. Toad!!

TOAD: I was laughin' about how funny these folks will look (LAFF) when they all fall in the river!

THEODORE: (BEAT) Fall in the . . . river?

TOAD: That's right, Theodore. I figured you'd change your mind about bein' big, so I brought some wishin' pond water in this leaf, so you can do your wishin' right in the middle of the river . . . (FADING) Now I'm goin' back home. I'll see you again . . . when you're . . . dissatisfied.

DUNKLE: Well, sir - Theodore turned around three times by the wishin' pond water in the leaf and he became little again!

DONNIE: But what about the people on his back?

DUNKLE: They grabbed the log that sleepy old Mr. Toad had been sunnin' himself on - and paddled to the riverbank, safe and sound!

DONNIE: And what about Theodore?

DUNKLE: He was happy to be little again.

DONNIE: You gonna tell me another story now, Uncle Dunkle?

DUNKLE: Donnie, like I said, you're jus' like Theodore . . .

DONNIE: Never satisfied!!

"UNCLE DUNKLE AND DONNIE AND WOOTSY"

DUNKLE: Hi, Donnie!

DONNIE: Hi.

DUNKLE: Come on up on the front porch and set yourself down!

DONNIE: O.K.

DUNKLE: Guess who's inside the house, talkin' to her Aunt Rapunzel!

DONNIE: You gonna tell me a story today?

DUNKLE: Guess who's inside talkin' to her Aunt Rapunzel!

DONNIE: Are ya?

DUNKLE: (ENTHUSED) Bet you can't guess!

DONNIE: Bet I don't wanna guess.

DUNKLE: You want me to tell ya?

DONNIE: You don't have to tell me. It's my cousin Wootsy.

DUNKLE: Correct!

DONNIE: I don't like it when she's here for the story tellin' . . .

DUNKLE: Why not?

DONNIE: You know 'why not!' She always gets real 'high tech' about the stories. She always puts her two cents in about the characters you make up. Things that aren't important. (PAUSE) Things that aren't germane.

DUNKLE: (BEAT) Germane? Where'd you pick up a word like 'germane?'

DONNIE: Does germane mean somethin'?

DUNKLE: Didn't you think it did?

DONNIE: I was just takin' a chance that it might. (GIGGLE)

DUNKLE: Well, Donnie . . . you lucked out!

DONNIE: You mean it really _does_ mean something?

DUNKLE: Sure does!! It means (CLEARS THROAT) 'Does it relate to the subject.'

DONNIE: What does _that_ mean?

DUNKLE: (LAYS IT OUT - LINEAR) It means 'Do I know what I'm talkin' about!'

DONNIE: Oh, you always know what you're talkin' about. You're the best storyteller I know.

DUNKLE: You're gonna make me blush . . . but I appreciate it! (BEAT) How many storytellers <u>do</u> you know . . . up close, I mean?

DONNIE: One.

DUNKLE: One?

DONNIE: (GIGGLE) <u>You</u>, Uncle Dunkle!

DUNKLE: (LAFF) I appreciate your loyalty . . . but it would have been more challenging if I coulda beat out some other storytellers . . . of classical status, I mean! (LAFF) . . . but you've aroused my curious. What put you on to the fact that Wootsy was inside the house?

DONNIE: Nothin' to it! Remember what you said? You said that 'she' was in the house with 'her' <u>Aunt Rapunzel</u>. (DRAMATIC) Now the plot thicks.

DUNKLE: Thickens.

DONNIE: That's what I said.

DUNKLE: Well, almost. Go on.

DONNIE: There's only <u>one</u> Aunt Rapunzel . . . and <u>one</u> Uncle Dunkle. <u>One</u> nephew and <u>one</u> niece. <u>One</u> Donnie and <u>one</u> Wootsy.

DUNKLE: (UP) Stop already!! (LAFF) I think you've '<u>one</u>' the argument!

DONNIE: (CHUCKLE) I suppose Wootsy is O.K.

DUNKLE: Of course she is!!

DONNIE: . . . for a girl.

DUNKLE: Don't get carried away! (LAFF) I'll just call her out here and after I tell you both a keen story . . . there's a good chance that your Aunt Rapunzel will bring us out some large warm bowls of turnip yogurt!

DONNIE: Yuk!

DUNKLE: Wootsy <u>loves</u> turnip yogurt!

DONNIE: Wootsy would! She can have mine. I'm a mustard fudge man, myself.

DUNKLE: I'll call her! (CLEARS THROAT) Wootsy! Wootsy!

WOOTSY: (OFF) Whatta you want, Uncle Dunkle?

DUNKLE: Guess who just came up on the front porch!

WOOTSY: (OFF) Your nephew?

DUNKLE: You're gettin' warm! What's his name? You've got one guess!

WOOTSY: (OFF) I hope I guess wrong. (GOOD PAUSE) Donnie?

DUNKLE: (UP - PLEASED) First guess out of the box was right! (LAFF) Yep, your cousin Donnie is here! Come on out here!

DONNIE: Hi, Wootsy.

WOOTSY: (COMES ON) Hi, Donnie.

DONNIE: 'Bye, Wootsy.

WOOTSY: 'Bye, Donnie.

(PAUSE)

DUNKLE: Is that all you've got to say to each other, Wootsy?

WOOTSY: I'm all talked out.

DONNIE: I'm no good at small talk . . . and there's no mark on a ruler small enough to show how small <u>this</u> talk is! (GIGGLE)

DUNKLE: I know you two are just ' around - but I want you to <u>get along</u>!!

WOOTSY: (BRISKLY) O.K. - see you later, Uncle Dunkle!

DONNIE: (BRISKLY) See you later.

DUNKLE: (UP) No!! Come back here! I didn't mean that kind of 'get along' . . . I meant 'get along' with each other! I'm sure you'll find lots of things in common if you think about it . . . <u>a little</u>!

WOOTSY: (SHORT PAUSE) Well, I certainly didn't come up with anything.

DONNIE: Me neither - I drew a complete blank, Uncle Dunkle.

DUNKLE: Did you both think about it . . . <u>a little</u>?

DONNIE & WOOTSY: Yes.

DUNKLE: Well, that 'little' was a lot 'littler' than the 'little' I had in mind! (CHANGE) Now be good sports, you two . . .

DONNIE & WOOTSY: (GIGGLE)

DUNKLE: Forget all these petty arguments and shake hands.

WOOTSY: O.K.

DONNIE: O.K.

DUNKLE: (UP) That's much better! Tell the truth, Wootsy. That wasn't so bad, was it?

WOOTSY: I'll see you later.

DUNKLE: (UP) Where you goin', Wootsy?

WOOTSY: I'm goin' to wash my hands.

DUNKLE: You're losin' the little bit of ground that you two had picked up! That wasn't very nice, Wootsy!

DONNIE: (UP) I'm not gonna wash my hands!

DUNKLE: Good for you, Donnie! Wanna tell me why?

DONNIE: Sure. I'm just not all that crazy about washin' my hands.

DUNKLE: (UP - TAKES OVER) O.K. you two!! I hereby declare a truce. I don't want any more of this silly talk!

WOOTSY: I think we're through.

DUNKLE: Both of you sit down on the swing!

DONNIE: (GIGGLES) Next to each other?

DUNKLE: Yes, next to each other!!

WOOTSY: It's a pretty small swing.

DUNKLE: Sit!!

DONNIE & WOOTSY: (GIGGLE)

DUNKLE: Now I'm gonna tell you a swell story. It's a true story. (CLEARS THROAT) Once upon a time there was a handsome little boy named . . .

DONNIE: (UP) Donnie.

DUNKLE: . . .and a little girl named . . .

WOOTSY: (UP) Wootsy - only not as pretty as me, I bet.

DUNKLE: Right! And they loved each other very much.

DONNIE: (GIGGLES) Yuk! I thought you said this was a true story!

WOOTSY: Sounds like a horror story.

DUNKLE: (PLOWS ON) . . . and wherever you found Wootsy, you found Donnie.

DONNIE: I hope they weren't too easy to find . . . (GIGGLE) not that I'd look very hard!

DUNKLE: One day a big, bad bully made some nasty remarks about Wootsy.

DONNIE: (UP) I like it! I like it! This is gettin' good!

DUNKLE: I'll ignore that! (UP) . . . and do you know why Donnie didn't like that?

DONNIE: Sure! Because he wanted to make the nasty remarks to Wootsy himself! (GIGGLE)

WOOTSY: (GIGGLES) Oh, you!!

DUNKLE: That isn't exactly the point I was tryin' to make. What I had in mind was this. (UP) . . .and it's a strong, structural story point.

DONNIE:	(YAWN) I can't wait.
WOOTSY:	I can probably guess what Donnie said.
DUNKLE:	I was gonna say that Donnie wanted to protect Wootsy from the bully.
DONNIE:	He should have protected the bully from Wootsy! (CHUCKLE)
WOOTSY:	That's what I thought Donnie was gonna say. (GIGGLE)
DUNKLE:	You two never change. You keep on insultin' each other . . . But you were doin' a lot of gigglin' there!! (LAFF)
WOOTSY:	It's the way we have fun, Uncle Dunkle. It doesn't mean anything . . .we just tease each other!
DONNIE:	I'm glad that Wootsy came over today. I had fun. Besides, my ballgame at school was canceled.
WOOTSY:	So?
DONNIE:	So seein' you was better than nothin'.

"UNCLE DUNKLE REVEALS ALL"

WOOTSY: Hi, Uncle Dunkle! Is Aunt Rapunzel home?

DUNKLE: Not right now. She was a few hours ago, though.

WOOTSY: Where is she now?

DUNKLE: She's over at the market . . . in the produce department.

WOOTSY: Doin' what?

DUNKLE: Well, you know how generous and outgoing your Aunt Rapunzel is.

WOOTSY: I know.

DUNKLE: Well, there was a fella over at the market who wanted to buy some wheat - but there wasn't any wheat in the market, so Mr. Bobble, who owns the market, asked your Aunt Rapunzel, who is very generous and outgoing, to help him out.

WOOTSY: You told me that . . . and anyway, I already knew it. (CHANGE) What did he want her to do?

DUNKLE: Did I tell you about the man who wanted to buy some wheat? WOOTSY: You just said he wanted to buy some wheat. You didn't tell me anything else about him.

DUNKLE: Did I tell you that Mr. Bobble didn't have any wheat?

WOOTSY: Yes. What did he want Aunt Rapunzel to do?

DUNKLE: He knew how clever your Aunt Rapunzel is with a needle and thread - and wanted her to sew some flour back into grains of wheat. And she's at the market now and that's what she's doin' . . .

WOOTSY: How long is it gonna take?

DUNKLE: Years, probably. The man wants three pounds of wheat.

WOOTSY: Do you think I believe this? Donnie might believe it but I don't. Why do you make up all these stories?

DUNKLE: because I'm a mean, old man. I'm handsome but hateful.

WOOTSY: Does Aunt Rapunzel know that you tell these crazy things about her?

DUNKLE: Not unless you tell her. You wouldn't snitch on me, would you?

WOOTSY: I used to think I wouldn't... but now I'm not sure. (BEAT) You love Aunt Rapunzel, don't you?

DUNKLE: Sure I do! If Aunt Rapunzel was on a little island, surrounded by crocodiles and there was no way for her to get off the island... do you know what I'd do?

WOOTSY: What?

DUNKLE: I'd feel awful sorry for her, I'll tell you that!!

WOOTSY: You're still making up stuff about Aunt Rapunzel, aren't you?

DUNKLE: Yes. But no man ever loved a woman as much as I love your Aunt Rapunzel. Ours is a great love story.

WOOTSY: How did you and Aunt Rapunzel meet?

DUNKLE: Well, I was the first mate on an old sailing ship and I'd gone around the Cape of Good Hope three times one summer.

WOOTSY: Why so many times?

DUNKLE: I fell asleep and I had the wheel locked in place - so the ship just kept goin' around and around.

WOOTSY: What has this got to do with your meeting Aunt Rapunzel?

DUNKLE: Nothing really. I met her at a dance. All the best lookin' gals in town were fighting for the chance to dance with me - but I chose your Aunt Rapunzel.

WOOTSY: Was she a good dancer?

DUNKLE: No, she was terrible.

WOOTSY: So what made you fall in love with her?

DUNKLE: She made the best mustard-fudge in town.

WOOTSY: Had you eaten mustard-fudge before?

DUNKLE: No . . . hers was the first I'd ever tasted.

WOOTSY: Then how'd you know it was the best?

DUNKLE: I talked myself into it. We went steady together for thirty years and then we got married together.

WOOTSY: But you've been <u>married</u> for thirty years.

DUNKLE: We must be older than I thought!

WOOTSY: Will you do something for me? And be serious about it.

DUNKLE: Anything your little heart desires.

WOOTSY: Tell me how you and Aunt Rapunzel <u>really</u> met.

DUNKLE: I'll put it down in my 'things to do' book. I'll give you a call when I'm ready to do it. That's fair, isn't it?

WOOTSY: I'll have to think about it . . . but I think I will.

DUNKLE: If you see Donnie, you could tell him about how your Aunt Rapunzel and I got to know each other and got married.

WOOTSY: Is Aunt Rapunzel down at the store sewing flour into grains? Or did you make that up?

DUNKLE: I made it up. (BEAT) She's in the house, takin' a snooze.

WOOTSY: I'm going in the house and say 'hello.'

DUNKLE: O.K. (CALLS) Look out for the crocodiles!!

NEW AUDIO BOOK TITLES FROM
BearManorAudio.com
AUDIO ON CD AND MP3 DOWNLOAD

ANIMATION

DAWS BUTLER'S UNCLE DUNKLE AND DONNIE
35 stories on four CDs, from the voice of Yogi Bear comes the world's first audio cartoon book, fully produced sound effects and original music, and performed by Daws Butler protege, NPR/XM radio theater producer and voice actor Joe Bevilacqua.

LONNIE BURR'S CONFESSIONS OF AN ACCIDENTAL MOUSEKETEER
Read by Lonnie Burr himself!

YABBA DABBA DOO: THE ALLAN REED STORY
Fred Flintstone's autobiography, voiced by radio's "Cartoon Carnival" host & voice actor Joe Bevilacqua.

HOLLYWOOD FILMS AND COMEDY

BILL MARX: SON OF HARPO SPEAKS
Growing up with the Marx Brothers, read Bill Marx!

BOB MILL'S THE LAUGH MAKERS
Behind the scenes, read by Bill Mills, who wrote for Bob Hope.

CORDIALLY YOURS, ANN SOTHERN
Read by NPR/XM radio theater and voice actress Lorie Kellogg.

DON AMECHE: THE KENOSHA COMEBACK KID
Read by NPR/XM radio theater producer and voice actor Joe Bevilacqua.

HOLD THAT JOAN: THE LIFE, LAUGHS AND FILMS OF JOAN DAVIS
Read by NPR/XM radio theater and voice actress Lorie Kellogg.

WALTER TETLEY: FOR CORN'S SAKE
Read by NPR/XM radio theater producer and voice actor Joe Bevilacqua.

RADIO DRAMA

IT'S THAT TIME AGAIN: THE NEW STORIES OF OLD-TIME RADIO
Fully produced sound effects and original music and performed by NPR/XM radio theater producer and voice actor Joe Bevilacqua.

www.ingramcontent.com/pod-product-compliance
Lightning Source LLC
Chambersburg PA
CBHW062007220426
43662CB00010B/1261